SOMETHING NEW
TO LEARN ABOUT
Cables

ARNALL-CULLIFORD KNITWEAR

Contents

SOMETHING NEW TO LEARN ABOUT **CABLES**

2

Contents

Introduction

JIM ARNALL-CULLIFORD

In another life, Jen and I studied chemistry. Both as undergraduates and as postgrads we had access to all sorts of textbooks. Some covered everything, but never in quite the depth we needed, whereas others were specific, but of such depth and size that they were intimidating to search through and pretty indigestible to read. The books we turned to most often weren't either of these, but slim volumes from a series. The *Oxford Chemistry Primers* were narrow enough in focus to be easy to read, but had sufficient depth that we could feel confident enough after reading them to tackle any problem. What I really appreciated were the worked examples that accompanied each section, to further illustrate the processes being described.

So what has this got to do with knitting? There are books that cover lots of techniques in a little detail and some that cover a particular technique in enormous detail. We think there's a space in everyone's bookshelves for a series of short books, each covering a particular aspect of knitting, that can be read through in their entirety as well as referred to in order to answer a specific question.

Whatever your experience of cables, we hope that there's something within this book to inspire you to try something different. Whether your cables need tracking, tidying or fixing, there are photo tutorials here backed up with video tutorials on our YouTube channel, and beautiful patterns that you can use to hone your newly acquired skills. So as well as showing you what to do, this book has plenty of help for those times when you look at your evening's progress and wonder what you were thinking about while you were knitting.

Join us, take the plunge and learn something new about cables.

SOMETHING NEW TO LEARN ABOUT **CABLES**

Chapter One

TUTORIALS:
BASIC CABLE TECHNIQUES

PROJECT
DESIGNED BY **Rachel Coopey**

BASIC CABLE TECHNIQUES

HOW TO CABLE

Simply put, a cable is a series of stitches worked out of order. Cables range from the simplest, where two equal sets of knit stitches are crossed over each other, to more complex combinations of knits and purls, where more than two groups of stitches are passed over or under each other. Cables can even be worked with increases, decreases and other stitches, bringing a rich variety of different effects. Most knitters start by learning a basic cable, such as 3/3 RC. This abbreviation means that 3 knit stitches cross 3 knit stitches, and the cross will lean to the right. The matching left-leaning cable is 3/3 LC.

You can choose whether to work with or without a cable needle for most basic cable stitches. Some people find it quicker to work without a cable needle, and others prefer to use one. There are no rules! It's a good idea to try both methods and see which you find easier. Cabling without a cable needle is easier with sticky yarns (non-superwash wool, as opposed to a slick cotton or silk) where the stitches won't easily drop when you take the needle out of them.

CABLING WITHOUT A CABLE NEEDLE

Cable instructions are generally given for using a cable needle, but once you have a feel for the purpose of the cable, it's fairly simple to adjust to not using a cable needle. If you work without a cable needle, you don't need to worry about misplacing the extra needle, and many knitters find it faster. Whatever your general preference, it's a handy skill to be able to call on when required.

WORKING 3/3 RC WITHOUT A CABLE NEEDLE

1 From the front, insert your right needle tip into the fourth, fifth and sixth stitches on your left needle.

2 Pinch the fabric below these stitches and then slip the left needle out of all 6 stitches. There are 3 stitches held on your right needle tip, and 3 stitches hanging free behind your right needle.

3 Carefully use your left needle tip to pick up the free stitches.

4 Return the 3 stitches on your right needle to your left needle.

5 Knit across all 6 stitches.

6 This produces a 3 over 3 right cross without the need for a cable needle.

WORKING 3/3 LC WITHOUT A CABLE NEEDLE

1 From the rear, insert your right needle tip into the fourth, fifth and sixth stitches on your left needle.

2 Pinch the fabric below these stitches and slip the left needle out of all 6 stitches. There are 3 stitches held on your right needle tip, and 3 stitches hanging free in front of your right needle.

3 Carefully use your left needle tip to pick up the free stitches.

4 Return the 3 stitches on your right needle to your left needle.

5 Knit across all 6 stitches.

6 This produces a 3 over 3 left cross without the need for a cable needle.

GENERAL INSTRUCTIONS ON HOW TO CABLE WITHOUT A CABLE NEEDLE

Having shown you how to work two specific cables without a cable needle, let's now look at how to work any cable where two sets of stitches cross. These instructions are general, but the photographs illustrate a 2/3 LPC.

1 Use the numbers in the cable abbreviation to tell you how many stitches are crossing over and under the fabric, and thus how many stitches are used in total. 2/3 LPC is 2 stitches passing over 3 stitches, and 5 stitches in total. 1/4 LPC is 1 stitch passing over 4 stitches, and also 5 stitches in total. Incidentally, this is why I use this particular cable nomenclature, since it's clear how many stitches are in each group. Many books would call both of these stitches T5F, which is ambiguous.

You then work out how many stitches are crossing from left to right, as these are the stitches you will be picking up with your right needle tip. In a left crossing cable, this will be the second number, as this is how many stitches are travelling under the fabric, and you will pick them up from the rear of the work.

In a right crossing cable it will be the first number, as this group of stitches is travelling over the fabric, so you will pick them up from the front of the work.

EXAMPLE CABLE ABBREVIATION SYMBOLS

 1/4 LPC slip 1 st to cable needle and hold at front, p4; k1 from cable needle

2/3 LPC slip 2 sts to cable needle and hold at front, p3; k2 from cable needle

2 Use your right needle tip to pick up the group of stitches that are crossing from left to right from the front of a right-leaning cable, or the back if your cable leans left.

3 Pinch the fabric below your cable, and slip your left needle out of all of the stitches involved in the cable.

4 Use your left needle to pick up the hanging stitch(es).

5 Return the stitches on the right needle to the left needle. You should now have your stitches crossing each other in the correct orientation.

6 Finally, work across the stitches in the pattern required. If the cable has the letters RC or LC, that means that all stitches are knitted. For cables with RPC or LPC the stitches travelling at the front of the fabric will be knitted and those passing behind will be purled. For RT or LT the stitches are all knitted through the back loop, and lastly for RPT or LPT the stitches travelling at the front of the fabric are knitted through the back loop, and those at the rear are purled.

7 Here we are working a 2/3 LPC so the first 3 stitches are purled as they are travelling at the rear of the fabric.

8 The second set of 2 stitches are knitted as they pass in front of the cable cross.

At first this process may seem fiddly or cumbersome, but as with all new skills, regular practice will help it to become more natural. Having a good understanding of how your stitches are travelling across your fabric will help increase your cabling confidence no end.

9 The 2/3 LPC cable has been completed without a cable needle.

TWO-STITCH CABLE SHORTCUTS

Small two-stitch cables can be done on the needles, without a cable needle, and are a great trick to have up your sleeve. Here are some basic 1/1 cables that you might like to use.

1/1 RC

Here we are ready to work a column of 1/1 RC cables.

1 From the front, insert your right needle tip into the second stitch on your left needle, as if to knit.

2 Wrap your yarn around the right needle tip and pull through a loop.

Basic Cable Techniques

3 Now insert your right needle tip into the first stitch on your left needle and knit it as normal.

4 Drop both stitches off your left needle at the same time.

ALTERNATE 1/1 RC METHOD

5 This completes the 1/1 RC carried out on the needles.

1 Insert your right needle tip into the first 2 stitches on your left needle, as if to k2tog.

2 Wrap the yarn around the right needle tip and pull through a loop, but do not drop the stitches off the needle.

3 Now insert your right needle tip into the first stitch on your left needle.

4 Knit this stitch as normal.

5 Drop both stitches off your left needle at the same time.

1/1 LC

1 From the rear, insert your right needle tip into the second stitch on your left needle.

2 Wrap the yarn around the right needle tip and pull through a loop.

3 Bring your right needle to the front of the work and knit into the first stitch as normal.

4 Drop both stitches off your left needle at the same time.

1/1 RPC

1 From the front, insert your right needle tip into the second stitch on your left needle, as if to knit.

2 Wrap your yarn around the right needle tip and pull through a loop.

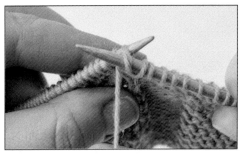

3 Bring the yarn to the front between your needle tips.

4 Now insert your right needle tip into the first stitch on your left needle and purl it as normal.

5 Drop both stitches off your left needle at the same time.

1/1 LPC

This cross is the trickiest to work on the needles without a cable needle. To make the manoeuvre manageable, the purl has to be worked through the back loop (the purl will be partially hidden by the knit so it won't be noticeable).

Alternatively, 1/1 LPC can be worked as 1/1 LC or you can work it without a cable needle, with a hanging stitch in the normal way.

◺◹ 1/1 LPC

1 From the rear, insert your right needle tip into the second stitch on the left needle to purl through the back loop.

2 Wrap the yarn around the right needle tip and pull through a loop.

3 Take the yarn to the back of the work between your needle tips.

4 Now insert your right needle tip into the first stitch on your left needle and knit it as normal.

5 Drop both stitches off your left needle at the same time.

Basic Cable Techniques

TRACKING ROWS IN CABLE PROJECTS

One of the things that slows me down the most in a cable project isn't the cabling itself, but rather it's knowing on which row or round to work the next cable! It's marginally easier when working on a flat project, since cables are generally only worked on right side rows, so it's not so tricky to tell the difference between 4 rows and 6 rows, and thus whether to work the next cable or not. However, when working in the round a difference of 1 round isn't so easy to spot until after a series of cables have been worked and you're a few rounds higher up the fabric, when the error becomes clearer.

In the following section I will refer only to rows of knitting, but it all applies equally to rounds.

Many knitters use a row counter to track their knitting, but I'm completely hopeless at remembering to click each row off, and I'm sure I'm not alone in also not being sure whether I have clicked or not! By far my favourite way of keeping track of rows in my knitting (and I use this for all types of projects, not just cables) is to use a running thread. It is simple to do, and it doesn't matter at all if you forget to run your marker as it is also easy to correct.

USING A RUNNING THREAD

1 Select a portion of your fabric that is relatively plain – stocking stitch or reverse stocking stitch is perfect. If possible, choose a section that is located after the start of the row, and before your first cable is to be worked. If the fabric has cables all over, then use the start of the row.

2 Cut a piece of waste yarn in a contrasting colour to your project. It should be longer than your intended piece of knitting. I use a mercerised white cotton as my waste yarn.

3 At the start of the row before working your first cable, when you reach your chosen point, lay your waste yarn over your knitting between your needles.

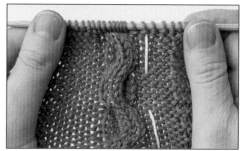

4 Continue to work in pattern. You will see that where you take your working yarn ready for the next stitch, the waste yarn is trapped through the fabric.

5 Having worked a few rows it is now straightforward to count the number of rows above the marker thread, by counting the purl bumps. The cable row was row 1, and you can count up from it.

6 If you forget to move your running marker (but remember to cable) then you can retrospectively sew the marker through the fabric in the correct place. This is also handy if you've already started a project and want to add a running marker later.

7 When you reach your next cable row, simply pass the thread from back to front (or front to back) between the needles and continue on your way.

I often use a running marker to keep track of rows in plain projects, to avoid having to count or measure too frequently. I pass the thread from one side of the project to the other, and can then count at a glance, only ever needing to count or measure up from the last marked point.

COUNTING ROWS ABOVE A CABLE

The other method that is handy, if you don't have waste yarn available, is to count the rows above the cable by locating the cross row.

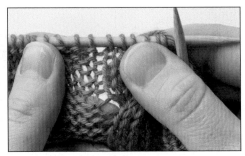

1 Use your fingers from the rear of the fabric to locate the small hole that forms when you cross your stitches.

2 Count the strands of yarn above this hole. The first row above the hole is the cable row.

3 Double check against your chart or instructions that your answer makes sense with the last row of knitting on your needles.

The following hat design by Rachel Coopey is the perfect project to try out some of these skills. Whether you are learning to cable for the first time, or you fancy trying to 1/1 cable on your needles, the Areto hat is a great way to experiment with any of the Basic Cable Techniques tutorials.

SOMETHING NEW TO LEARN ABOUT **CABLES**

PROJECT
ARETO HAT

by Rachel Coopey

PROJECT **ARETO HAT**

YARN
Coop Knits Socks Yeah! DK (75% superwash merino wool, 25% nylon; 112m [122yds] per 50g skein)
Hat shown in Aeacus (210); 2 (2, 3) x 50g skeins

NEEDLES AND NOTIONS
1 set 3.5mm [US 4] circular needles, 40cm [16in] long, or double-pointed needles, or needle size required to match tension
1 set 4mm [US 6] circular needles, 40cm [16in] long, and double-pointed needles, or needle size required to match tension
Stitch markers
Cable needle (optional)

TENSION
32 sts and 36 rounds to 10cm [4in] over unstretched 2x2 rib, using smaller needles
Cable A panel (20 sts) to 6.5cm [2½in], using larger needles
30 rounds to 10cm [4in] over cable panel and rib, using larger needles

ABBREVIATIONS
Cable abbreviations can be found in the key for the chart.
A full abbreviations list can be found on pages 86–87.

PATTERN NOTES
This hat is worked in the round from the brim up. Crown shaping is worked into the cable panels. The deep rib brim is folded up for wear. Since the hat is knitted in the round, all chart rows are read from right to left. The charted cable panels are also provided as written instructions.

SIZES
Small (Medium, Large)
To fit approximate head circumference:
51 (56, 61) cm [20 (22, 24) in]
Unstretched hat circumference at brim:
37.5 (44, 50) cm [14¾ (17¼, 19¾) in]
Unfolded hat from brim to crown: 27cm [10¾in]
The hat is designed for a slouchy fit. The body cable and rib patterns are *very* stretchy.

HAT

1 BRIM
Cast on 120 (140, 160) sts and join to work in the round, taking care not to twist. Pm for start of round.

Round 1: *P2, k2, rep from * to end.
Rep last round a further 21 times.

For charted instructions move to step 2, for written instructions move to step 3.

2 HAT BODY – CHARTED INSTRUCTIONS
CHARTS APPEAR ON FOLLOWING PAGE
Change to larger needles.
Next round (inc): *[P2, k2] 1 (2, 3) times, p2, kfb, 1/1 LPC, 1/1 RPC, M1P, k1, [p2, k2] 3 times; rep from * to end. *10 sts inc; 130 (150, 170) sts.*

Round 1: *[P2, k2] 1 (2, 3) times, p2, work across 20 sts from row 1 of chart A; rep from * to end.
Last round sets chart patterns and rib.
Working next row of charts each time, cont in pattern as set until chart A has been completed.
Now rep chart rows 9–16 twice more.

For charted crown shaping instructions move to step 4, for written crown shaping instructions move to step 5.

3 HAT BODY – WRITTEN INSTRUCTIONS
Change to larger needles.
Next round (inc): *[P2, k2] 1 (2, 3) times, p2, kfb, 1/1 LPC, 1/1 RPC, M1P, k1, [p2, k2] 3 times; rep from * to end. *10 sts inc; 130 (150, 170) sts.*

Round 1: *[P2, k2] 1 (2, 3) times, p2, k1, p2, k2, p2, k1, [p2, k2] 3 times; rep from * to end.

Round 2: *[P2, k2] 1 (2, 3) times, p2, [1/1 LPC, 1/1 RPC] twice, [p2, k2] twice, p1, 2/1 RC; rep from * to end.
Round 3: *[P2, k2] 1 (2, 3) times, p3, k2, p2, k2, p3, k2, p2, k1, k3; rep from * to end.
Round 4: *[P2, k2] 1 (2, 3) times, p2, [1/1 RPC, 1/1 LPC] twice, [p2, k2] twice, 2/1 RC, k1; rep from * to end.
Round 5: *[P2, k2] 1 (2, 3) times, p2, k1, p2, k2, p2, k1, p2, k2, p2, k6; rep from * to end.
Round 6: *[P2, k2] 1 (2, 3) times, p2, [1/1 LPC, 1/1 RPC] twice, p2, k2, p2, k1, 2/1 RPC, k2; rep from * to end.
Round 7: *[P2, k2] 1 (2, 3) times, p3, k2, p2, k2, p3, k2, p2, k3, p1, k2; rep from * to end.
Round 8: *[P2, k2] 1 (2, 3) times, p2, [1/1 RPC, 1/1 LPC] twice, p2, k2, p2, 2/1 RPC, p1, k2; rep from * to end.
Round 9: Rep round 1.
Round 10: *[P2, k2] 1 (2, 3) times, p2, [1/1 LPC, 1/1 RPC] twice, p2, k2, [p1, 2/1 RC] twice; rep from * to end.
Round 11: *[P2, k2] 1 (2, 3) times, p3, k2, p2, k2, p3, k2, [p1, k3] twice; rep from * to end.
Round 12: *[P2, k2] 1 (2, 3) times, p2, [1/1 RPC, 1/1 LPC] twice, p2, k2, [2/1 RC, k1] twice; rep from * to end.
Round 13: *[P2, k2] 1 (2, 3) times, p2, k1, p2, k2, p2, k1, p2, k10; rep from * to end.
Round 14: *[P2, k2] 1 (2, 3) times, p2, [1/1 LPC, 1/1 RPC] twice, p2, [k1, 2/1 RPC] twice, k2; rep from * to end.
Round 15: *[P2, k2] 1 (2, 3) times, p3, k2, p2, k2, p3, [k3, p1] twice, k2; rep from * to end.
Round 16: *[P2, k2] 1 (2, 3) times, p2, [1/1 RPC, 1/1 LPC] twice, p2, [2/1 RPC, p1] twice, k2; rep from * to end.

Now rep rounds 9–16 twice more.

For charted crown shaping instructions move to step 4, for written crown shaping instructions move to step 5.

Chapter 1

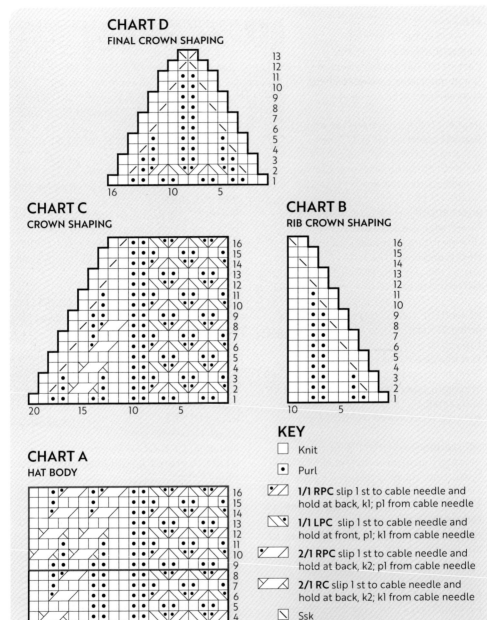

CHART D
FINAL CROWN SHAPING

CHART C
CROWN SHAPING

CHART B
RIB CROWN SHAPING

CHART A
HAT BODY

KEY

☐	Knit
⊡	Purl
⤢	**1/1 RPC** slip 1 st to cable needle and hold at back, k1; p1 from cable needle
⤡	**1/1 LPC** slip 1 st to cable needle and hold at front, p1; k1 from cable needle
⤢	**2/1 RPC** slip 1 st to cable needle and hold at back, k2; p1 from cable needle
⤢	**2/1 RC** slip 1 st to cable needle and hold at back, k2; k1 from cable needle
◺	Ssk
◹	K2tog
☐	Pattern repeat

SOMETHING NEW TO LEARN ABOUT **CABLES**

4 CROWN SHAPING –
   CHARTED INSTRUCTIONS

During crown shaping, as the circumference decreases, you may find it more comfortable to change to double-pointed needles.

LARGE SIZE

Round 1: *P2, work across 10 sts from row 1 of chart B, p2, work 20 sts from row 1 of chart C; rep from * to end.

Last round sets chart pattern. Working next row of charts each time, cont in pattern as set until both charts have been completed. *80 sts dec; 90 sts remain.*

MEDIUM SIZE

Round 1: *[P2, k2] twice, p2, work 20 sts from row 1 of chart C; rep from * to end.

Last round sets chart pattern. Working next row of chart each time, cont in pattern as set until row 9 of chart C has been completed. *20 sts dec; 130 sts remain.*

Round 10: *P2, work 6 sts from row 10 of chart B, p2, work across row 10 of chart C; rep from * to end.

Last round sets chart pattern. Working next row of charts each time, cont in pattern as set until chart C has been completed. *40 sts dec; 90 sts remain.*

SMALL SIZE

Round 1: *P2, k2, p2, work 20 sts from row 1 of chart C; rep from * to end.

Last round sets chart C pattern. Working next row of chart each time, cont in pattern as set until chart C has been completed. *40 sts dec; 90 sts remain.*

ALL SIZES

Round 17: *P2, work 16 sts from row 1 of chart D; rep from * to end.

Last round sets chart D pattern. Working next row of chart each time, cont in pattern as set until chart D has been completed. *70 sts dec; 20 sts remain.*

Partial round: Remove marker for start of round, p1, replace marker for start of round.

Round 30 (dec): *Ssk, k2tog; rep from * to end. *10 sts dec; 10 sts remain.*

Break yarn and pull through remaining sts. Move to step 6.

Chapter 1

SOMETHING NEW TO LEARN ABOUT **CABLES**

5 CROWN SHAPING –
WRITTEN INSTRUCTIONS

During crown shaping, as the circumference decreases, you may find it more comfortable to change to double-pointed needles.

SMALL AND MEDIUM SIZES

Round 1: *[P2, k2] 1 (2, –) times, p2, k1, p2, k2, p2, k1, [p2, k2] 3 times; rep from * to end.

Round 2 (dec): *[P2, k2] 1 (2, –) times, p2, [1/1 LPC, 1/1 RPC] twice, p2, k2, p1, 2/1 RC, p1, k2tog, k1; rep from * to end. *5 sts dec; 125 (145, –) sts remain.*

Round 3: *[P2, k2] 1 (2, –) times, p3, k2, p2, k2, p3, k2, p1, k3, p1, k2; rep from * to end.

Round 4 (dec): *[P2, k2] 1 (2, –) times, p2, [1/1 RPC, 1/1 LPC] twice, p2, k2, 2/1 RC, k1, k2tog, k1; rep from * to end. *5 sts dec; 120 (140, –) sts remain.*

Round 5: *[P2, k2] 1 (2, –) times, p2, k1, p2, k2, p2, k1, p2, k8; rep from * to end.

Round 6 (dec): *[P2, k2] 1 (2, –) times, p2, [1/1 LPC, 1/1 RPC] twice, p2, k1, 2/1 RPC, k1, k2tog, k1; rep from * to end. *5 sts dec; 115 (135, –) sts remain.*

Round 7: *[P2, k2] 1 (2, –) times, p3, k2, p2, k2, p3, k3, p1, k3; rep from * to end.

Round 8 (dec): *[P2, k2] 1 (2, –) times, p2, [1/1 RPC, 1/1 LPC] twice, p2, 2/1 RPC, p1, k2tog, k1; rep from * to end. *5 sts dec; 110 (130, –) sts remain.*

Round 9: *[P2, k2] 1 (2, –) times, p2, k1, p2, k2, p2, k1, [p2, k2] twice; rep from * to end.

LARGE SIZE

Round 1: *P2, [k2, p2] 3 times, k1, p2, k2, p2, k1, [p2, k2] 3 times; rep from * to end.

Round 2 (dec): *P2, k1, ssk, p1, [k2, p2] twice, [1/1 LPC, 1/1 RPC] twice, p2, k2, p1, 2/1 RC, p1, k2tog, k1; rep from * to end. *10 sts dec; 160 sts remain.*

Round 3: *P2, k2, p1, k2, p2, k2, p3, k2, p2, k2, p3, k2, p1, k3, p1, k2; rep from * to end.

Round 4 (dec): *P2, k1, ssk, [k2, p2] twice, [1/1 RPC, 1/1 LPC] twice, p2, k2, 2/1 RC, k1, k2tog, k1; rep from * to end. *10 sts dec; 150 sts remain.*

Round 5: *P2, k4, p2, k2, p2, k1, p2, k2, p2, k1, p2, k8; rep from * to end.

Round 6 (dec): *P2, k1, ssk, k1, p2, k2, p2, [1/1 LPC, 1/1 RPC] twice, p2, k1, 2/1 RPC, k1, k2tog, k1; rep from * to end. *10 sts dec; 140 sts remain.*

Round 7: *P2, k3, p2, k2, p3, k2, p2, k2, p3, k3, p1, k3; rep from * to end.

Round 8 (dec): *P2, k1, ssk, p2, k2, p2, [1/1 RPC, 1/1 LPC] twice, p2, 2/1 RPC, p1, k2tog, k1; rep from * to end. *10 sts dec; 130 sts remain.*

Round 9: *P2, [k2, p2] twice, k1, p2, k2, p2, k1, [p2, k2] twice; rep from * to end.

SMALL SIZE

Round 10 (dec): *P2, k2, p2, [1/1 LPC, 1/1 RPC] twice, p2, k2, p1, k2tog, k1; rep from * to end. *5 sts dec; 105 sts remain.*

Round 11: *P2, k2, p3, k2, p2, k2, p3, k2, p1, k2; rep from * to end.

Round 12 (dec): *P2, k2, p2, [1/1 RPC, 1/1 LPC] twice, p2, k2, k2tog, k1; rep from * to end. *5 sts dec; 100 sts remain.*

Round 13: *P2, k2, p2, k1, p2, k2, p2, k1, p2, k4; rep from * to end.

Round 14 (dec): *P2, k2, p2, [1/1 LPC, 1/1 RPC] twice, p2, k1, k2tog, k1; rep from * to end. *5 sts dec; 95 sts remain.*

Round 15: *P2, k2, p3, k2, p2, k2, p3, k3; rep from * to end.

Round 16 (dec): *P2, k2, p2, [1/1 RPC, 1/1 LPC] twice, p2, k2tog, k1; rep from * to end. *5 sts dec; 90 sts remain.*

MEDIUM AND LARGE SIZES

Round 10 (dec): *P2, k1, ssk, p1, k2, p2, [1/1 LPC, 1/1 RPC] twice, p2, k2, p1, k2tog, k1; rep from * to end. *10 sts dec; 120 sts remain.*

Round 11: *P2, k2, p1, k2, p3, k2, p2, k2, p3, k2, p1, k2; rep from * to end.

Chapter 1

Round 17: *P2, k2, p2, k1, p2, k2, p2, k1, p2, k2; rep from * to end.

Round 18 (dec): *P2, k1, ssk, p1, [1/1 LPC, 1/1 RPC] twice, p1, k2tog, k1; rep from * to end. *10 sts dec; 80 sts remain.*

Round 19: *P2, k2; rep from * to end.

Round 20 (dec): *P2, k1, ssk, p1, k2, p2, k2, p1, k2tog, k1; rep from * to end. *10 sts dec; 70 sts remain.*

Round 21: *P2, k2, p1, k2, p2, k2, p1, k2; rep from * to end.

Round 22 (dec): *P2, k1, ssk, k2, p2, k2, k2tog, k1; rep from * to end. *10 sts dec; 60 sts remain.*

Round 23: *P2, k4; rep from * to end.

Round 24 (dec): *P2, k1, ssk, k1, p2, k1, k2tog, k1; rep from * to end. *10 sts dec; 50 sts remain.*

Round 25: *P2, k3; rep from * to end.

Round 26 (dec): *P2, k1, ssk, p2, k2tog, k1; rep from * to end. *10 sts dec; 40 sts remain.*

Round 27: *P2, k2; rep from * to end.

Round 28 (dec): *P2, k1, ssk, k2tog, k1; rep from * to end. *10 sts dec; 30 sts remain.*

Round 29 (dec): *P2, k2tog, ssk; rep from * to end. *10 sts dec; 20 sts remain.*

Partial round: Remove marker for start of round, p1, replace marker for start of round.

Round 30 (dec): *Ssk, k2tog; rep from * to end. *10 sts dec; 10 sts remain.*

Break yarn and pull through remaining sts.

6 FINISHING
Weave in all ends. Soak your hat in lukewarm water with wool wash for 20–30 minutes. Squeeze out excess water. Lay flat to dry, taking care not to overstretch the ribbing, or dry over a hat form or balloon or stuff with plastic bags. Leave to dry.

Round 12 (dec): *P2, k1, ssk, k2, p2, [1/1 RPC, 1/1 LPC] twice, p2, k2, k2tog, k1; rep from * to end. *10 sts dec; 110 sts remain.*

Round 13: *P2, k4, p2, k1, p2, k2, p2, k1, p2, k4; rep from * to end.

Round 14 (dec): *P2, k1, ssk, k1, p2, [1/1 LPC, 1/1 RPC] twice, p2, k1, k2tog, k1; rep from * to end. *10 sts dec; 100 sts remain.*

Round 15: *P2, k3, p3, k2, p2, k2, p3, k3; rep from * to end.

Round 16 (dec): *P2, k1, ssk, p2, [1/1 RPC, 1/1 LPC] twice, p2, k2tog, k1; rep from * to end. *10 sts dec; 90 sts remain.*

Chapter Two

FIXING CABLES

It happens. You're working away perfectly happily on a project, and you glance down at the fabric in front of you, and clear as day, there's a cable going the wrong way! "How could I not have spotted it at the time?" I hear you cry! Please rest assured that we have all done it, and you don't necessarily need to rip out all those rows of knitting.

In this chapter I'm going to walk you through a series of different methods for correcting mistakes in your cable stitches. Choosing which method to use will depend on both your confidence in dealing with the method, and the placement and type of error. Not all mistakes need correcting, and it's often worth remembering that we see the errors in our knitting far more than anyone else does – unless we choose to point out the errors ourselves!

DROPPING A WHOLE ROPE CABLE

Where a series of cables are placed directly on top of each other, it is a simple job to drop the stitches involved in the cable and correct the cross. In the following example, a panel using alternating 3/3 RC and 3/3 LC cables has been worked incorrectly 4 rows back. A 3/3 LC has been worked instead of a 3/3 RC.

1 Work until you reach the start of the cable rope.

2 Carefully slip all of the stitches involved in the cable rope off your left needle.

3 Use a needle or crochet hook to unravel the previous row of stitches.

4 Unravel these stitches down to the mis-crossed row. The incorrect cable cross should spring open when you reach the row that needs correcting.

5 Slip the two sets of stitches onto separate cable needles or double-pointed needles.

6 Correct the cross by passing one set of stitches behind the other, and slipping all of the stitches to one spare needle.

7 Use a crochet hook to pick up the first of the dropped stitches. You may find it helpful to anchor the needle holding the remaining stitches by threading it through some nearby fabric.

8 Pick up each of the stitches in turn, keeping some tension in the unravelled yarn, so that you pick up the threads in the correct order.

9 Once all of the columns of stitches are picked up, you may find that some stitches are a bit uneven.

10 If stretching the fabric in both directions doesn't work, then use a spare needle to carefully pull any slack from loose stitches across the row.

11 Work over the cable rope as normal. It should be almost impossible to tell where the error was.

DROPPING PART OF A ROPE CABLE

Where the rope cable involves two evenly split sets of stitches, you don't need to drop the entire rope. So for example, in a rope of 3/3 RC cables, there are two sets of 3 stitches. If we have worked a 3/3 LC by mistake, just one of the strands of 3 stitches can be dropped in order to correct the cross. In the following swatch a panel of stacked 3/3 RC cables has been worked incorrectly 10 rows back, where a 3/3 LC has been worked by mistake. If you have a choice of which strand to drop, then choose the strand that does most of its crosses at the front of the fabric.

1 Work until you reach the start of the cable.

2 Slip the first set of stitches off your left needle (in this case it's just 3 stitches).

3 Unravel the set of stitches down to the mis-crossed row.

4 Once you reach the mis-crossed cable, pick up the dropped stitches on a spare needle.

5 Carefully move the stitches to the opposite side of the fabric in order to correct the cable, by passing them through the hole left by the cross.

6 Check that you still have all of your stitches safely on your needles at the other side of the work.

7 And bring them behind the still-knitted strand, ready to pick back up.

8 Use a crochet hook to pick up the first stitch, making sure to use the correct strand of unravelled yarn for each row.

9 As you pick the stitch up over a cable row, try to ensure that it doesn't get too over-stretched, by holding the fabric firmly.

10 Particularly when you only have one stitch remaining to be picked up, it's worth anchoring your spare needle in the surrounding fabric so that the needle doesn't fall out of your stitch.

11 Pick up the final stitch.

12 Your picked up cable may seem a little uneven. In which case, give the fabric a good tug in both directions, and it should even out.

13 It should now be almost impossible to tell that there was ever a mistake in your knitting.

DROPPING A CABLE STRAND IN A MORE COMPLEX DESIGN

Sometimes a mis-crossed cable appears in a more complex design, where the cables move stitches across the surface of the fabric. In this situation you need to identify where the mis-crossed stitches now appear on your needles. The easiest solution is to look at the chart.

For example, if the 2/2 LC on row 12 of diagram 1 has been mistakenly worked as a right cross and we are now working from row 18, you can trace the path of the two pairs of stitches involved in the cable to work out where they now appear on the needles. One of the pairs has been worked straight up, without any further movement. The other pair has passed through the 2/2 LPC and 2/2/2 RPC on rows 14 and 16 respectively. To fix this cable, I would drop stitches 7 and 8, since they will drop straight down to the desired row.

But what if the mis-crossed cable is the 2/2 LC on row 6 of diagram 2 and we have now completed row 13 of the chart? Both of the pairs of stitches from the mis-crossed cable have passed through a subsequent cable. Depending on the complexity of the design, you might decide that it's worth un-knitting a round or two of work in order to make fixing the error more straightforward. If you took this chart back to row 11, you could then drop the right-hand pair straight down. Or you can drop the strand through the cable above as follows:

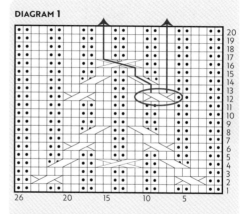

DIAGRAM 1

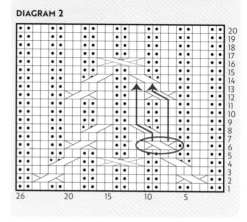

DIAGRAM 2

1 Work until you reach the group of stitches you wish to drop.

2 Slip the desired stitches (here we are dropping 2 knit stitches) off your left needle tip.

3 Use a spare needle to pull the yarn out of each row of stitches.

4 Continue to unravel down to the row of the mis-cross, and slip the stitches onto a spare needle.

5 Poke the spare needle holding the stitches through to the opposite side of the fabric.

6 Make sure you have all your stitches safely on your needles still, and that they aren't twisted.

7 Bring the stitches back to the right side of the fabric, below the ladder of unravelled yarn, thus completing the cross.

8 Anchor your spare needle on the right side of the work, ready to pick up the dropped stitches.

9 Slip the first stitch to a crochet hook and pick up each of the stitches in turn, making sure to use the correct strand of unravelled yarn for each row.

10 Make sure that the stitches are picked up from the correct side of the fabric as they pass through the cable above.

11 Repeat steps 9 and 10 to pick up any remaining stitches.

12 Once you have finished picking up the dropped strand of stitches, check that everything looks correct before you continue to follow your pattern.

USING EMBROIDERY

Sometimes a cable will be too far down, or have too many crosses on top of it, to make dropping stitches the best solution. Perhaps you didn't spot the mistake until you had completed the piece you were knitting? In this situation, correcting the cross by embroidering over the fabric is the easiest solution. One of the benefits of this approach is that you can have a few tries, and pull out your stitches if you aren't happy with them. Since you aren't actually changing the fabric underneath the embroidery, it is a very forgiving method. The basic embroidery stitch that is used is chain stitch.

In the following swatch a panel of stacked 3/3 RC cables has been worked incorrectly 10 rows back, where a 3/3 LC has been worked by mistake.

1 Identify a row of stitches just below the incorrect cable. It may be helpful to run a contrasting thread along this row, so that you don't get lost as you are sewing.

2 Thread some waste yarn through a row of stitches above the cross. Visualise how the stitches should look when they are correctly crossed. You will be adding two stitches on the surface of the fabric in each stitch column. So in this case, a total of 6 embroidered stitches.

3 Thread a blunt tapestry needle with a good length of your main yarn (I am using a contrasting colour here to make it easier to see my stitches).

4 The left half of the lower row of stitches needs to cross to the right half of the upper row. Pass the tapestry needle from the wrong side to the right side of the fabric, through the centre of the right-hand stitch from the group to be crossed, on the row below the cable.

SOMETHING NEW TO LEARN ABOUT **CABLES**

5 Pass the needle back down through the same stitch in order to create a small loop on the surface of the fabric. This is your first replacement stitch. Now pass your needle back up, between where the first stitch has been created and the right-hand stitch from the group above, and pass your needle through the loop you have made.

6 Run the needle under the base of the first stitch on the row above the cross, catching both strands of yarn, and mimicking the knitted stitch below it.

7 Pass the needle back down through the loop you created on the surface of the fabric, in the same place where you just came up.

8 Start the next column of stitches by bringing your tapestry needle up through the bottom of the next stitch along on the row below the cross.

9 Continue to work as described in steps 4 to 7, until all the columns of stitches have been corrected.

11 Remove any contrasting running threads, if you used them. This swatch shows how the corrected fabric looks when the same colour yarn is used.

Correcting by embroidery isn't the most invisible fix, but in a fabric with many crosses, it won't be noticeable (unless you choose to point it out!). It is definitely worth trying an embroidery fix in the first instance, since it's easy enough to remove if you aren't happy with how it looks.

SNIPPING AND GRAFTING

If your incorrect cable is a long way down, and somewhere really noticeable, then sometimes the only solution is to take your scissors to your knitting. Not in a drastic, "I'm throwing this in the bin!" way, but in a controlled and strategic manner. This is the cable-correcting version of adding an afterthought heel or thumb. If you think of it in this way, it feels slightly less alarming to be cutting your work.

    The aim of this process is to isolate the stitches on each side of the cross, and then to unravel back a central row of stitches, re-cross the cable, and graft the stitches back together.

1 Use your finger to find the hole where the cable crossed, and in this way, to identify the row of cable stitches (the strand of yarn above your finger is the row required).

2 Picking up the right-hand leg of each stitch, run a piece of waste yarn through the stitches of the row below the cross. On the row above the cross, skip the first stitch on the right, and pick up the first purl stitch on the left of the cable instead.

3 Identify a stitch in the centre of the cross row, and carefully snip through just one stitch.

4 Unravel the ends of your main yarn, leaving the stitches above and below safely on waste yarn, ensuring that the stitches on the row below the cross are completely free.

5 Take these ends to the wrong side of the fabric and roughly weave them in (you can tidy them neatly later, this is just so that you don't worry about anything else unravelling).

6 Slip the two sets of stitches on the row below onto two separate needles (or cable needles).

7 Re-cross the stitches in the correct orientation. Slip all of the crossed stitches onto one needle and return the stitches above the cross to another needle.

8 Leaving a tail of yarn, graft the two sets of stitches together, starting with the set-up step as normal (pass the needle through the first stitch on the front needle purlwise and on the rear needle knitwise).

9 Graft your stitches loosely to begin with. Then adjust the tension of the stitches in the graft line so that it matches the surrounding fabric.

Fixing Cables

10 You will notice that there is a hole at the right-hand end of the graft. Fix this by threading the tail back onto a needle and passing it through the bottom stitch.

11 Pass the needle from left to right under the right-hand leg of the right-most stitch on the row above the cross.

12 And pass the needle back down through the right-most stitch on the row below the cross, to the wrong side of the fabric.

13 Weave in the remaining ends, tidying any corners if required. It should be almost impossible to tell that there was ever a mistake in the cable.

With an intertwining cable panel on the back of the hand, my Otrera Mittens and Mitts are a great project on which to practise fixing cable mistakes (not that you will make any, of course!).

PROJECT
OTRERA MITTENS AND MITTS
by Jen Arnall-Culliford

PROJECT **OTRERA MITTENS**

YARN
Coop Knits Socks Yeah! DK (75% fine superwash merino wool, 25% nylon; 112m [122yds] per 50g skein)
Mittens shown in Demeter (209); 2 (2, 3) x 50g skeins
Mitts shown in Morpheus (206); 2 x 50g skeins in all sizes

NEEDLES AND NOTIONS
1 set 3mm [US 2.5] double-pointed needles, or your preferred needles for working small circumferences in the round, or needle size required to match tension
Small quantity of waste yarn for holding stitches
Stitch markers
Cable needle (optional)

TENSION
A dense fabric is required to ensure that your mittens are hard-wearing.
28 sts and 36 rounds to 10cm [4in] over stocking stitch
Unstretched cable panel (26 sts) measures 5cm [2in]

ABBREVIATIONS
Cable abbreviations can be found in the key for the chart.
A full abbreviations list can be found on pages 86–87.

SIZES
Small (Medium, Large)
To fit approximate hand circumference above thumb: 16–19 (19–22, 22–25) cm [6¼–7½ (7½–8¾, 8¾–9¾) in]
Unstretched mitten and mitt circumference above thumb: 15 (18, 20.5) cm [6 (7, 8¼) in]
Mittens finished length: 28.5 (28.5, 32.5) cm [11¼ (11¼, 12¾) in]
Mitts finished length: 21 (21, 23.5) cm [8¼ (8¼, 9¼) in]

PATTERN NOTES
Both mittens and mitts are knitted in the round. The thumb is worked with gusset increases before the stitches are left on hold to be completed later. The cable panel is worked up the back of the hand, and is mirrored on left and right hands. Since the mittens are knitted in the round, all chart rows are read from right to left. The charted cable panel is also provided as written instructions.

MITTENS

1 RIGHT MITTEN – CUFF
Using the long-tail method, cast on 48 (56, 64) sts and join to work in the round, taking care not to twist. Pm for start of round.

SMALL AND LARGE SIZES
Round 1: *K2, p2; rep from * to end.

MEDIUM SIZE
Round 1: *P2, k2; rep from * to end.

ALL SIZES
Rep last round a further 19 (19, 23) times.

2 RIGHT MITTEN – HAND
Written instructions for chart A can be found adjacent to the chart.

Reading all chart rows from right to left, work hand as foll:
Round 1: K2 (4, 6), work across 26 sts from row 1 of chart A, k0 (2, 4), pm, k2, pm, knit to end.
Round 2 (inc): K2 (4, 6), work across 26 sts from row 2 of chart A, k0 (2, 4), M1L, slm, k2, slm, M1R, knit to end. *2 sts inc; 50 (58, 66) sts.*

Rounds 3–5: K2 (4, 6), work across 26 sts from next row of chart A, knit to marker, slm, k2, slm, knit to end.
Round 6 (inc): K2 (4, 6), work across 26 sts from next row of chart A, knit to marker, M1L, slm, k2, slm, M1R, knit to end. *2 sts inc.*
Rep last 4 rounds a further 7 (7, 8) times. *16 (16, 18) sts inc; 66 (74, 84) sts.*
You should have completed chart A row 14 (14, 18) for the second time.
Work 2 further rounds in pattern (without increases).

Next round: K2 (4, 6), work across 26 sts from next row of chart A, k3 (5, 7), slip next 14 (14, 16) sts to waste yarn for thumb (leaving markers in place), using the backwards loop method, cast on 2 sts, knit to end. *54 (62, 70) sts remain.*

Next round: K2 (4, 6), work across 26 sts from next row of chart A, knit to end.
†Work in pattern as set by last round for a further 32 (32, 38) rounds (until chart row 10 (10, 20) is complete for the fourth time).

3 TOP OF RIGHT MITTEN
Round 1 (dec): K1, ssk, k0 (1, 3), p1 (2, 2), [k2, p2] 5 times, k2, p1 (2, 2), k0 (1, 3), k2tog, k1, pm, knit to end. *2 sts dec; 52 (60, 68) sts remain.*
Round 2: K2 (3, 5), p1 (2, 2), [k2, p2] 5 times, k2, p1 (2, 2), k2 (3, 5), slm, knit to end.
Round 3 (dec): K1, ssk, work in rib as set to 3 sts before marker, k2tog, k1, slm, knit to end. *2 sts dec.*
Round 4: K2, work in rib as set to 2 sts before marker, k2, slm, knit to end.
Rounds 5 & 6: Rep rounds 3 & 4. *2 sts dec; 48 (56, 64) sts remain.*
Round 7 (dec): K1, ssk, work in rib as set to 3 sts before marker, k2tog, k1, slm, k1, ssk, knit to last 3 sts, k2tog, k1. *4 sts dec.*
Round 8: Rep round 4.
Rounds 9–12: Rep round 7. *16 sts dec; 28 (36, 44) sts remain.* ‡

SMALL AND LARGE SIZES
Round 13 (dec): *K1, ssk, [k2tog, skk] 2 (–, 4) times, k2tog, k1, slm; rep from * once more. *12 (–, 20) sts dec; 16 (–, 24) sts remain.*

MEDIUM SIZE
Round 13 (dec): *K1, ssk, [ssk, k2tog] 3 times, k2tog, k1, slm; rep from * once more. *16 sts dec; 20 sts remain.*

4 THUMB

Starting at centre of base of thumb, pick up and knit 2 sts from cast-on edge, and knit across 14 (14, 16) thumb sts from holder (keeping markers in place), pick up and knit a further 2 sts from base of thumb. *18 (18, 20) sts.* Pm for start of round.

Round 1: Ssk, knit to marker, M1L, slm, k2, slm, M1R, knit to last 2 sts, k2tog.

Rounds 2–4: Knit.

Rep last 4 rounds a further 4 (4, 5) times.

Next round (dec): Ssk, knit to marker, remove marker, k1, pm, k1, remove marker, knit to last 2 sts, k2tog. *2 sts dec; 16 (16, 18) sts remain.*

Next round (dec): *Ssk, knit to 2 sts before marker, k2tog, slm; rep from * once more. *4 sts dec; 12 (12, 14) sts remain.*

Next round (dec): *Ssk, knit to 2 sts before marker, k2tog, slm; rep from * once more. *4 sts dec; 8 (8, 10) sts remain.*

LARGE SIZE

Next round (dec): *Ssk, knit to 2 sts before marker, k2tog, slm; rep from * once more. *4 sts dec; 6 sts remain.*

ALL SIZES

Break yarn and pull through remaining sts.

5 LEFT MITTEN – CUFF

Using the long-tail method, cast on 48 (56, 64) sts and join to work in the round, taking care not to twist. Pm for start of round.

SMALL AND LARGE SIZES

Round 1: *P2, k2; rep from * to end.

MEDIUM SIZE

Round 1: *K2, p2; rep from * to end.

ALL SIZES

Rep last round a further 19 (19, 23) times.

ALL SIZES

Turn mitten inside out, and join 8 (10, 12) back of hand sts to 8 (10, 12) palm sts using a three-needle cast off as foll:

Arrange your stitches so that you have 8 (10, 12) back of hand sts on one needle and 8 (10, 12) palm sts on a second needle, with the needle tips both pointing in the same direction, adjacent to the working yarn. Use a third needle to knit together the first stitch from the back of hand and palm needles (1 st on right needle). *Knit together the first stitch from the back of hand and palm needles (2 sts on right needle). Cast off 1 st on right needle. Rep from * until all back of hand and palm sts are worked. Break yarn and pull through remaining st.

CHART A RIGHT HAND
WRITTEN INSTRUCTIONS
Worked over 26 sts and 20 rounds.
Round 1: [P2, k2] 6 times, p2.
Round 2: P2, 2/2 LC, [k2, p2]
3 times, k2, 2/2 RC, p2.
Round 3: P2, k6, [p2, k2] twice,
p2, k6, p2.
Round 4: P2, k2, 2/2 LPC, p2,
2/2/2 LPC, p2, 2/2 RPC, k2, p2.
Round 5: Rep round 1.
Round 6: P2, k2, p2, 2/2 LC, k2,
p2, k2, 2/2 RC, p2, k2, p2.
Round 7: P2, k2, p2, [k6, p2]
twice, k2, p2.
Round 8: [P2, k2] twice, 2/2 LPC,
p2, 2/2 RPC, [k2, p2] twice.
Rounds 9–11: Rep round 1.
Rounds 12–14: Rep rounds 6–8.
Round 15: Rep round 1.
Round 16: P2, [k2, p2] twice,
2/2/2 LPC, [p2, k2] twice, p2.
Rounds 17–20: Rep round 1.

KEY

☐ Knit

⊡ Purl

2/2 RC slip 2 sts to cable needle and hold at back, k2; k2 from cable needle

2/2 LC slip 2 sts to cable needle and hold at front, k2; k2 from cable needle

2/2 RPC slip 2 sts to cable needle and hold at back, k2; p2 from cable needle

2/2 LPC slip 2 sts to cable needle and hold at front, p2; k2 from cable needle

2/2/2 LPC slip 2 sts to cable needle and hold in front, slip next 2 sts to a second cable needle and hold at back, k2; p2 from back cable needle; k2 from front cable needle

CHART A RIGHT HAND

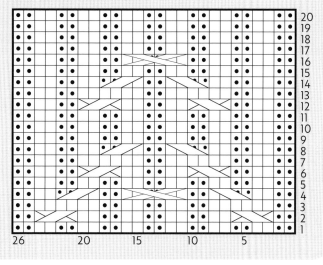

6 LEFT MITTEN – HAND

Written instructions for chart B can be found adjacent to the chart.

Reading all chart rows from right to left, work hand as foll:
Round 1: K18 (22, 26), pm, k2, pm, k0 (2, 4), work across 26 sts from row 1 of chart B, k2 (4, 6).
Round 2 (inc): Knit to marker, M1L, slm, k2, slm, M1R, k0 (2, 4), work across 26 sts from row 2 of chart B, k2 (4, 6). *2 sts inc; 50 (58, 66) sts.*

Rounds 3–5: Knit to marker, slm, k2, slm, knit to last 28 (30, 32) sts, work across 26 sts from next row of chart B, k2 (4, 6).
Round 6 (inc): Knit to marker, M1L, slm, k2, slm, M1R, knit to last 28 (30, 32) sts, work across 26 sts from next row of chart B, k2 (4, 6). *2 sts inc.*
Rep last 4 rounds a further 7 (7, 8) times. *16 (16, 18) sts inc; 66 (74, 84) sts.*
You should have completed chart B row 14 (14, 18) for the second time.
Work 2 further rounds in pattern (without increases).

Next round: Knit to 6 (6, 7) sts before marker, slip next 14 (14, 16) sts to waste yarn for thumb (leaving markers in place), using the backwards loop method, cast on 2 sts, knit to last 28 (30, 32) sts, work across 26 sts from next row of chart B, k2 (4, 6). *54 (62, 70) sts remain.*

Next round: Knit to last 28 (30, 32) sts, work across 26 sts from next row of chart B, k2 (4, 6).
**Work in pattern as set by last round for a further 32 (32, 38) rounds (until chart row 10 (10, 20) is complete for the fourth time).

7 TOP OF LEFT MITTEN

Round 1 (dec): K24 (28, 32), pm, k1, ssk, k0 (1, 3), p1 (2, 2), [k2, p2] 5 times, k2, p1 (2, 2), k0 (1, 3), k2tog, k1. *2 sts dec; 52 (60, 68) sts remain.*
Round 2: Knit to marker, slm, k2 (3, 5), p1 (2, 2), [k2, p2] 5 times, k2, p1 (2, 2), k2 (3, 5).
Round 3 (dec): Knit to marker, slm, k1, ssk, work in rib as set to last 3 sts, k2tog, k1. *2 sts dec.*
Round 4: Knit to marker, slm, k2, work in rib as set to last 2 sts, k2.
Rounds 5 & 6: Rep rounds 3 & 4. *2 sts dec; 48 (56, 64) sts remain.*
Round 7 (dec): K1, ssk, knit to 3 sts before marker, k2tog, k1, slm, k1, ssk, work in rib as set to last 3 sts, k2tog, k1. *4 sts dec.*
Round 8: Rep round 4.
Rounds 9–12: Rep round 7. *16 sts dec; 28 (36, 44) sts remain.*

Complete Left Mitten as Right Mitten from ‡ in step 3 and all of step 4.

8 FINISHING

Weave in all ends, closing any gaps around the base of the thumb if necessary. Soak your mittens in lukewarm water with wool wash for 20–30 minutes. Squeeze out excess water. Lay flat to dry, taking care to arrange the ribbing so that it lies straight, or dry over mitten blockers.

CHART B LEFT HAND
WRITTEN INSTRUCTIONS
Worked over 26 sts and 20 rounds.
Round 1: [P2, k2] 6 times, p2.
Round 2: P2, 2/2 LC, [k2, p2]
3 times, k2, 2/2 RC, p2.
Round 3: P2, k6, [p2, k2] twice,
p2, k6, p2.
Round 4: P2, k2, 2/2 LPC, p2,
2/2/2 RPC, p2, 2/2 RPC, k2, p2.
Round 5: Rep round 1.
Round 6: P2, k2, p2, 2/2 LC, k2,
p2, k2, 2/2 RC, p2, k2, p2.
Round 7: P2, k2, p2, [k6, p2]
twice, k2, p2.
Round 8: [P2, k2] twice, 2/2 LPC,
p2, 2/2 RPC, [k2, p2] twice.
Rounds 9–11: Rep round 1.
Rounds 12–14: Rep rounds 6–8.
Round 15: Rep round 1.
Round 16: P2, [k2, p2] twice,
2/2/2 RPC, [p2, k2] twice, p2.
Rounds 17–20: Rep round 1.

KEY

☐ Knit

⊡ Purl

2/2 RC slip 2 sts to cable needle and hold at back, k2; k2 from cable needle

2/2 LC slip 2 sts to cable needle and hold at front, k2; k2 from cable needle

2/2 RPC slip 2 sts to cable needle and hold at back, k2; p2 from cable needle

2/2 LPC slip 2 sts to cable needle and hold at front, p2; k2 from cable needle

2/2/2 RPC slip 4 sts to cable needle and hold at back, k2; slip left-hand 2 sts from cable needle to left needle, p2; k2 from cable needle

CHART B LEFT HAND

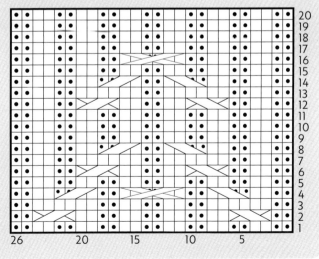

SOMETHING NEW TO LEARN ABOUT **CABLES**

MITTS

1 RIGHT MITT – CUFF
Work as Mittens step 1 (page 43).

2 RIGHT MITT – HAND
Work as Mittens step 2 to † (page 43).
Work in pattern as set by last round for a
further 12 rounds (until chart A row 10 (10,
14) is complete for the third time).

3 RIGHT MITT – EDGING
SMALL AND LARGE SIZES
Round 1 (dec): K2, [p2, k2] 8 (–, 10) times,
p2tog, p1, k2, [p2, k2] 2 (–, 4) times, p1, p2tog,
k2, p2. *2 sts dec; 52 (–, 68) sts remain.*
Round 2: *K2, p2; rep from * to end.
Rep last round a further 4 times.
Cast off all sts in rib.

MEDIUM SIZE
Round 1 (dec): [P2, k2] 10 times, p2tog, p1, k2,
[p2, k2] 3 times, p1, p2tog, k2. *2 sts dec; 60 sts
remain.*
Round 2: *P2, k2; rep from * to end.
Rep last round a further 4 times.
Cast off all sts in rib.

4 RIGHT MITT – THUMB
Starting at centre of base of thumb, pick up
and knit 2 sts from cast-on edge, and knit
across 14 (14, 16) thumb sts (keeping markers
in place), pick up and knit a further 2 sts
from base of thumb. *18 (18, 20) sts.* Pm for
start of round.
Round 1: Ssk, knit to marker, M1L, slm, k2,
slm, M1R, knit to last 2 sts, k2tog.
Rounds 2–4: Knit.
Rep last 4 rounds once (once, twice) more.

SMALL AND MEDIUM SIZES
Round 21 (dec): Ssk, knit to marker, remove
marker, k2, remove marker, knit to last 2 sts,
k2tog. *2 sts dec; 16 (16, –) sts remain.*

ALL SIZES
Next round: *K1, p2, k1; rep from * to end.
Rep last round a further 3 times.
Cast off all sts in rib.

5 LEFT MITT – CUFF
Work as Mittens step 5 (page 44).

6 LEFT MITT – HAND
Work as Mittens step 6 to ** (page 46).
Work in pattern as set by last round for a
further 12 rounds (until chart B row 10 (10, 14)
is complete for the third time).

7 LEFT MITT – EDGING
Small and Large Sizes
Round 1 (dec): P2, k2, p2tog, p1, [k2, p2] 2 (–,
4) times, k2, p1, p2tog, [k2, p2] 8 (–, 10) times,
k2. *2 sts dec; 52 (–, 68) sts remain.*

Round 2: *P2, k2; rep from * to end.
Rep last round a further 4 times.
Cast off all sts in rib.

MEDIUM SIZE
Round 1 (dec): K2, p2tog, p1, [k2, p2] 3 times,
k2, p1, p2tog, [k2, p2] 10 times. *2 sts dec; 60
sts remain.*
Round 2: *K2, p2; rep from * to end.
Rep last round a further 4 times.
Cast off all sts in rib.

8 LEFT MITT – THUMB
Work as step 4 (page 49).

9 FINISHING
Work as Mittens step 8 (page 46).

Chapter Three

ADVANCED CABLE TECHNIQUES

AXIS CABLES

Up to this point, all of the cables we have discussed use two sets of stitches crossing each other. When a third set of stitches is introduced, an axis cable can be created, where a set of stitches on each side crosses over a central set that remains constant – the cables cross around an axis. Axis cables have many possible variations, with the main ones being whether the central stitches are visible at the front of the work (on the left of the swatch below), or hidden at the back (on the right of the swatch below).

The most prevalent axis cables are those where the central group is hidden at the rear of the work, while a group on each side crosses the front. This type of cable is typified by the 2/2/2 LPC and RPC worked in my Otrera Mittens, as well as the 2/1/2 RPC found in Lucy's Pleione Cowl and Blanket. The central number in the abbreviation tells you how many stitches are in the central (or axis) group, and following the same nomenclature as for the cables previously, RPC and LPC are knit stitches crossing over a purl stitch axis (RC and LC would be axis cables where all of the stitches are knitted).

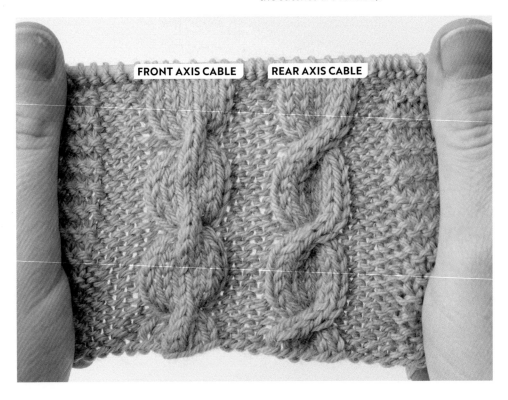

FRONT AXIS CABLE   REAR AXIS CABLE

SOMETHING NEW TO LEARN ABOUT **CABLES**

WORKING AN RPC AXIS CABLE

This swatch is ready to work a 2/1/2 RPC axis cable.

1 Looking at the cable abbreviation, ignore the first number, and slip the sum of the second two numbers to a cable needle held at the rear of the work, e.g. for 2/1/2 RPC you will slip 3 sts to your cable needle.

2 Knit the number of stitches given by the first number in the abbreviation.

3 Slip the axis stitch(es) (the central number) from the left-hand end of the cable needle back to the left needle.

4 Purl the axis stitch(es).

5 Knit the remaining stitches on the cable needle.

WORKING AN LPC AXIS CABLE

6 You have now produced an axis cross where the two columns of knit stitches swap sides, while the purl stitches remain central.

This swatch is ready to work a 2/1/2 LPC axis cable. Two cable needles are required for left crossing axis cables.

1 Slip the first number of stitches in the abbreviation to a cable needle held at the front of the work.

2 Slip the second number of stitches in the abbreviation (the axis stitch(es)) to a cable needle held at the back of the work.

3 Knit the third number of stitches from the left needle.

4 Return the stitch from the back cable needle to the left needle.

SOMETHING NEW TO LEARN ABOUT **CABLES**

5 Purl this stitch.

6 Knit the stitches from the cable needle at the front.

7 You have completed an axis cable where the two columns of knit stitches cross, leaning to the left, a central purl axis.

FAUX AXIS CABLES

What about if you're in a hurry? Or you really can't face juggling two cable needles? Well, it is also possible to fake an axis cable! To do so, you treat the three-way cable as a two-way cable, working the stitches across the front correctly, but without bothering to switch the stitches at the rear of the work. The finished cables have a slightly different appearance. The knit stitches passing at the back of the work aren't angled in the same way as on a true axis cable, but this may be an acceptable trade off for the ease in working a faux cable.

True axis cables.

Faux axis cables.

FAUX RPC AXIS CABLES

These instructions are general, but the photographs show a faux 2/1/2 RPC cable.

1 Slip the sum of the first two numbers in the cable abbreviation (3 stitches in this example) to a cable needle held at the rear of the work. These are the rear knit stitches and the central purl stitch(es).

2 Knit the third number of stitches from the left needle (in this case, 2 stitches).

3 From the cable needle, purl the central number of stitches from the cable abbreviation (in this case, 1 stitch).

4 Knit the remaining stitches from the cable needle. As you work these stitches you will notice that your knits and purls aren't lined up with the stitches below them. In a proper axis cable, the knits and purls would continue to be lined up in continuous columns.

5 You've completed a faux axis cable. Once a few more rows have been worked, the slight misalignment of the rear strand of knit stitches will become clearer.

FAUX LPC AXIS CABLES

These instructions are general, but the photographs show a faux 2/1/2 LPC cable.

1 Slip the first number of stitches from the cable abbreviation to cable needle held at the front of the work (in this case, 2 stitches).

2 Knit the third number of stitches from the cable abbreviation, from the left needle.

3 Purl the middle number of stitches from the cable abbreviation, from the left needle. You will notice that in steps 2 and 3 your knits and purls aren't lined up with the stitches below them.

4 Knit the stitch(es) from the cable needle.

5 You've completed a faux axis cable. Once a few more rows have been worked, the slight misalignment of the rear strand of knit stitches will become clearer.

> *Whether you choose to work a true axis cable, or its faux cousin, be sure to stick with your chosen method within a project. They do look slightly different from each other and inconsistency would lead your project to appear less polished.*

TIDYING BAGGY STITCHES

This is a really common problem in both ribbing and cables. When you switch from a knit to a purl, the last knit stitch can look loose in comparison to its neighbours.

Whilst the problem manifests itself in the last knit stitch, the solution is found in the first purl stitch. The knit stitch tends to look loose because of the path the yarn takes around the needle when transitioning from knit to purl. There are three possible fixes, and I would suggest that you knit a sample and see which works best for you.

PURL MORE TIGHTLY

The first fix is the simplest. When you work the first two purl stitches after a section of knit, be sure to give the yarn an extra tug to help to tighten that area of fabric. Many people do this automatically, and never even notice that they are doing so. It's a simple fix, but in the long term, anything that causes tension in your hands while knitting also carries the risk of increased repetitive strain injuries. So I would advise caution in taking this approach.

Both the second and third solutions solve the problem by forcing the purl stitch to use less yarn, and thus tighten up the neighbouring knit stitch. These approaches work really well, but require practice in order to make them feel natural.

COMBINATION KNITTING SOLUTION

All of the instructions in this book assume that you are wrapping the yarn around your needle in order to mount your stitches with the leading (or right-hand) leg at the front of the needle. This is the so-called Western method.

Combination knitting involves wrapping the yarn around the needle in the opposite direction when purling. This mounts the purl stitches with the leading leg at the rear of the needle. Working the first purl stitch in this way gives the yarn a shorter path and thus tightens up both the knit and purl stitches. The downside is that you then need to remember to work this stitch through the back loop on the following row or round, so that it isn't twisted.

1 Knit the final stitch of the rib or cable.

2 Bring the yarn to the front and insert the needle ready to purl the next stitch.

3 Wrap the yarn the opposite way round the needle to normal, and complete the stitch.

4 Work the next stitch in the normal way.

WORKING BACK ACROSS THE TWISTED STITCH ON A WRONG SIDE ROW

5 You can see that the first purl stitch is now mounted in the opposite direction.

When you work along the next row, remember to knit this stitch through the back loop so that the stitch remains untwisted.

WORKING BACK ACROSS THE TWISTED STITCH ON THE RIGHT SIDE (IN THE ROUND)

1 When you come to the twisted purl stitch you need to work it through the back loop.

2 You also need to wrap the yarn around in the "wrong" direction. This is because you need to untwist the previous row's stitch AND work the next one so that it uses less yarn.

SLIPPED STITCH SOLUTION

Like the combination approach, this fix to those baggy rib and cable stitches requires you to work the stitches differently on the following round. This requires some practice, but isn't inherently difficult to do.

1 Knit the final stitch of the rib or cable.

2 Bring the yarn to the front, but slip the next stitch purlwise, rather than purling it.

WORKING BACK ACROSS THE SLIPPED STITCH ON A WRONG SIDE ROW

3 Work the next stitch in the normal way. You can see that the first purl stitch has a bar of yarn in front of it – this is the yarn that will later be used to make the purl stitch. This bar is shorter than the yarn would be if the stitch had been simply purled.

1 Work the following row until you reach the stitch which was slipped. Use your left needle tip to pick up the bar lying below the slipped stitch from front to back.

2 Lift the slipped stitch over the bar of yarn, thus making the purl stitch from the row below.

3 Continue to work along the row as normal.

WORKING BACK ACROSS THE SLIPPED STITCH ON THE RIGHT SIDE (IN THE ROUND)

1 With your working yarn held out of the way at the front of the work, insert your right needle into the next stitch (the slipped stitch) on the left needle as if to purl, and under the bar of yarn sitting in front of the stitch.

2 Use the left needle tip to pull the slipped stitch over the bar of yarn, thus completing the purl from the previous round.

3 That first purled stitch is now on the right needle, and the purl from the previous round has been "caught up", but the stitch hasn't been worked on this round. Work the next stitch on the left needle in the normal way. This creates a new bar along the bottom of that first purl stitch.

Continue to work in this way until you reach the last round that is worked in this rib or cable pattern (or the final round before the work is cast off). In this final row you will need to resolve the purl from the row below as in the instructions above and then work the purl for the current row as well. This is the only row or round where the purl is both resolved and worked.

OPENING AND CLOSING A KNOT CABLE

While many cable patterns work vertically, with the cables growing out of some sort of ribbing, it is also possible to commence a cable pattern from an almost horizontal starting point, and thus to create closed-loop or knot-like cables. These are used to great effect in Lucy Hague's Pleione Cowl and Blanket, where the cables create a star-shaped closed-knot pattern. The inner points of the star grow from a background of reverse stocking stitch, and the two knit columns diverge from an almost invisible

starting point. This is achieved using a 1 into 5 increase, and at the outer points of the star a 5 into 1 decrease seamlessly closes the ends of the knit 2 columns.

In a 1 into 5 increase, the original stitch remains in the centre, and 2 new stitches are created on each side. When subsequent rows are knitted above, particularly when the 2 stitches on each side are cabled away from the centre stitch, this increase gives the impression of a horizontal row of unbroken stitches.

Ⅴ **1 INTO 5**

1 With the yarn at the rear of the work, insert your right needle tip between the first and second stitches on your left needle.

2 Wrap the yarn around your right needle and pull a loop through.

3 Slip the first stitch on your left needle to your right needle.

4 Insert your left needle between the first and second stitches on your right needle.

Advanced Cable Techniques

5 Wrap the yarn around your left needle.

6 Pull that loop through. You can see 1 new stitch on your left needle, and a new stitch and the original stitch on your right needle.

7 Slip the first stitch on your right needle back to your left needle (this was the original stitch).

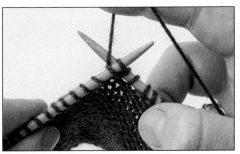

8 Insert the right needle tip between the first and second stitches on your left needle, wrap the yarn around and pull a loop through.

9 Slip the first stitch on your left needle onto your right needle.

10 Insert the left needle between the first two stitches on your right needle, wrap the yarn around and pull a loop through.

11 You can now see the two new stitches on the left needle, as well as the original stitch and two new stitches on the right needle tip.

12 Slip 2 stitches from your left needle to your right needle.

13 You can now see that you've completed a 1 into 5 increase, where there are two new stitches created each side of a central stitch.

CLOSING A KNOT CABLE

To close the top of a cabled knot or loop, you will need to work a 5 into 1 or 5 into 1[p] decrease. This works best when the two columns of knit stitches have been cabling towards each other on previous rows. Once the decrease is complete, it gives the impression of a horizontal row of unbroken stitches, and mirrors the 1 into 5 increase.

⚠ **5 INTO 1**

The following swatch is ready to work a 5 into 1 decrease.

1 Slip next 3 stitches to right needle.

2 Insert the left needle into the second stitch on the right needle.

3 Pass the second slipped stitch over first stitch on right needle and off the needle.

4 Slip 1 stitch from right needle back to the left needle.

5 Insert the right needle into the second stitch on the left needle.

6 Pass second stitch on left needle over the first stitch and off the needle.

7 Slip 1 stitch from left needle to right needle.

8 Pass the second stitch on the right needle over the first stitch and off the needle.

9 Slip the remaining stitch on right needle back to left needle.

10 Pass the second stitch on left needle over first stitch and off the needle.

11 Knit the remaining stitch.

12 This completes your 5 into 1 decrease.

5 INTO 1 [P]

1 Work steps 1–10 in the same way as for a 5 into 1 decrease.

2 Purl remaining stitch.

3 Once the row or round is complete, the top of the knit strands appear to be joined horizontally.

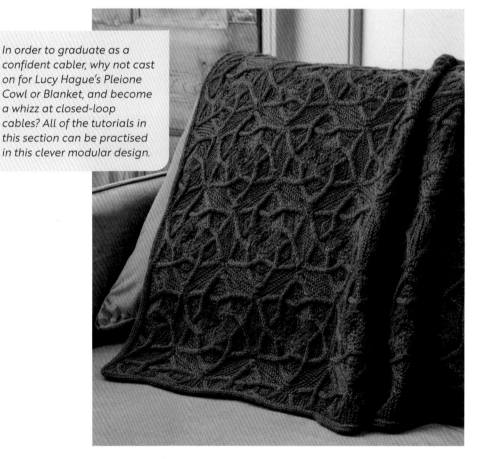

In order to graduate as a confident cabler, why not cast on for Lucy Hague's Pleione Cowl or Blanket, and become a whizz at closed-loop cables? All of the tutorials in this section can be practised in this clever modular design.

SOMETHING NEW TO LEARN ABOUT **CABLES**

PROJECT
**PLEIONE COWL
AND BLANKET**
by Lucy Hague

SIZES

Short cowl: 30.5cm [12in] wide with 49.5cm [19½in] circumference
Long cowl: 23cm [9in] wide with 74.5cm [29¼in] circumference
Blanket: 76cm x 74.5cm [30in x 29¼in]

YARN

Coop Knits Socks Yeah! DK (75% fine superwash merino wool, 25% nylon; 112m [122yds] per 50g skein)
Short cowl shown in Anemoi (204); 4 x 50g skeins
Long cowl shown in Minos (202); 4 x 50g skeins
Blanket shown in Astra Planeti (203); 12 x 50g skeins

Each hexagon requires approx. 44m [48yds] of DK-weight yarn.

NEEDLES AND NOTIONS

1 set 4mm [US 6] double-pointed needles, or your preferred needles for working small circumferences in the round, or needle size required to match tension
Optional 4mm [US 6] circular needle, 30cm [12in] long, or needle size required to match tension
1 set 4mm [US 6] circular needles, 60–80cm [24–32in] long, for joining and edging, a second set may be required if you prefer to arrange stitches for joining on separate needles
Waste yarn or stitch holders
Small quantity of waste yarn and crochet hook for provisional cast-on (blanket only)
Cable needle
1 stitch marker

TENSION

22 sts and 29 rounds over 10cm [4in] in stocking stitch, after washing and blocking
Each hexagon measures approx. 15cm [6in] in width measured from centre of a straight edge across centre to opposite centre of straight edge, and approx. 16.5cm [6½in] in width measured from one point across centre to opposite point, after washing and blocking
It is strongly recommended that you check your tension after knitting, washing and blocking your first hexagon.

ABBREVIATIONS

5 into 1[p] Slip next 3 stitches to right needle, pass second slipped stitch over first stitch on right needle and off needle. Slip stitch from right needle back to left needle and pass second stitch on left needle over first stitch and off needle. Slip stitch from left needle to right needle and pass second stitch over first stitch and off needle. Slip remaining stitch on right needle back to left needle and pass second stitch on left needle over first stitch and off needle; purl remaining stitch (4 stitches decreased)

1 into 5 With yarn at back of work, *insert right needle between first 2 stitches on left needle, wrap yarn around right needle and pull through to make a stitch, slip first stitch on left needle to right needle, insert left needle between first 2 stitches on right needle, wrap yarn around left needle and pull through to make a stitch*, slip first stitch on right needle to left needle; rep from * to * once more, slip 2 stitches from left needle to right needle (4 stitches increased)

Cable abbreviations can be found in the key for the chart.
A full abbreviations list can be found on pages 86–87.

PATTERN NOTES

Both the cowls and blanket are worked in separate hexagonal pieces, which are joined together. The hexagons are joined in strips and half-hexagons are knitted on at the edges, working the cable pattern in the opposite direction to the full hexagons. At the ends of the blanket are rows of half-hexagons to give a straight edge. The cowls and blanket are both edged with i-cord to give a neat finish.

SPECIAL TECHNIQUES

Photo tutorials for the following techniques can be found within this book.

1 into 5 (page 62)

5 into 1[p] (page 67)

2/1/2 RPC (page 53)

The following video tutorials may be found on our website at www.acknitwear.co.uk/ something-new-to-learn-about-cables

Pinhole cast-on method

1 into 5 increase

5 into 1[p] decrease

Grafting (Kitchener stitch)

3-needle cast-off method

Crochet provisional cast on

JOINING NOTES

All hexagons are joined either by grafting or using the 3-needle cast-off method. For most of the short edge joins, you will be able to use the tails left from each hexagon. For the longer edge joins, and where necessary, use a new length of yarn.

To prepare to graft your hexagons together, hold both sets of stitches parallel on needles with the tips pointing to the right and the right sides of the work outermost. To prepare to join your hexagons using the 3-needle cast-off method, hold both sets

of stitches parallel on needles with the tips pointing to the right and the wrong sides of the work outermost.

Whichever method you use, take care not to pull the yarn too tight on the first few stitches, as this could over-tighten the previous stitches remaining on waste yarn or a holder, and make it hard to join them later. When the join is complete, pull the end through the final stitch, and leave it hanging so that it can be used later to neaten any holes.

KEY

- ☐ Knit on RS, purl on WS
- ☐• Purl on RS, knit on WS
- Ⓜ M1 on RS, M1P on WS
- Ⓜ M1P on RS
- Ⓨ Kfb on RS
- Ⓨ Kfbf on RS
- ☑ Ssk on RS, ssp on WS
- ☑ P2tog on WS
- Ⓚ K3tog on RS
- ☑ P2tog on RS
- ☑ Ssp on RS
- Ⓐ 5 into 1[p]
- Ⓨ 1 into 5
- Ⓥ Sl1 pwise wyif
- ☐ Pattern repeat

- Ⓥ|Ⓥ Remove marker, sl 2 pwise wyib, replace marker
- ☐☐ K2, apart from final repeat, when these 2 sts are not worked (they are used in the 5 into 1 on the next round)
- **2/1 RPC** slip 1 st to cable needle and hold at back, k2; p1 from cable needle
- **2/1 LPC** slip 2 sts to cable needle and hold at front, p1; k2 from cable needle
- **2/2 RPC** slip 2 sts to cable needle and hold at back, k2; p2 from cable needle
- **2/2 LPC** slip 2 sts to cable needle and hold at front, p2; k2 from cable needle
- **2/1/2 RPC** slip 3 sts to cable needle and hold at back, k2; return left-hand st from cable needle to left needle, p1; k2 from cable needle
- **2/3 LPC** slip 2 sts to cable needle and hold at front, p3; k2 from cable needle
- **2/3 RPC** slip 3 sts to cable needle and hold at back, k2; p3 from cable needle

CHART B
SIDE HALF-HEXAGONS

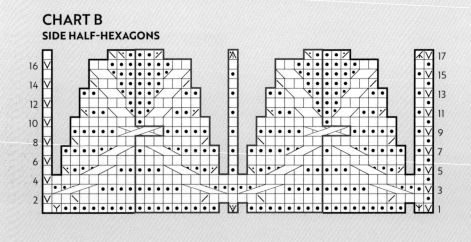

COWL

1 CAST ON FOR HEXAGONS
Using the pinhole method, cast on 6 sts and arrange the sts on your needles as desired, pm and join to work in the round. Turn work so that the purl bumps from the cast-on round are facing you.

Round 1: Purl to end.
Round 2 (inc): [P1, M1P] 6 times. *6 sts inc; 12 sts.*
Rounds 3 & 4: Purl to end.
Round 5 (inc): [P1, M1P] 12 times. *12 sts inc; 24 sts.*
Rounds 6–8: Purl to end.
Round 9 (inc): [P1, M1P, p3, M1P] 6 times. *12 sts inc; 36 sts.*
Rounds 10 & 11: Purl to end.

For charted instructions move to step 2, for written instructions move to step 3.

2 WORK HEXAGON CABLE PATTERN
   CHARTED INSTRUCTIONS
In the following section, swap to a short circular needle if required, once you have sufficient sts.
Round 12 (inc): Work across row 12 of chart A 6 times. *36 sts inc; 72 sts.*
Last round sets chart A pattern. Cont to work from chart A until chart row 28 is complete. Take care on round 13 to only work the two slipped sts once at the start of the round, and on round 27, ending 2 sts before the end of the round (see chart for full details). *36 sts inc; 108 sts.*

Break yarn, leaving tail approx. 40cm [16in] and sl all sts to waste yarn or a stitch holder.

Make a further 5 hexagons (both cowls use the same number of complete hexagons).

Move to step 4.

CHART A
BASIC HEXAGONS

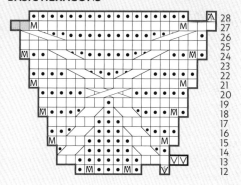

3 WORK HEXAGON CABLE PATTERN WRITTEN INSTRUCTIONS

In the following section, swap to a short circular needle if required, once you have sufficient sts.

Round 12 (inc): [1 into 5, p1, M1P, p3, M1P, p1] 6 times. *36 sts inc; 72 sts.*

Round 13: Remove marker, sl2 pwise wyib, replace marker, k3, [p7, k5] 5 times, p7, k2.

Round 14: [P1, 2/1 LPC, p5, 2/1 RPC] 6 times.

Round 15 (inc): [K1, M1, k3, p5, k3, M1] 6 times. *12 sts inc; 84 sts.*

Round 16: P3, [2/1 LPC, p3, 2/1 RPC, p5] 5 times, 2/1 LPC, p3, 2/1 RPC, p2.

Round 17: K6, [p3, k11] 5 times, p3, k5.

Round 18 (inc): [P1, M1P, p3, 2/1 LPC, p1, 2/1 RPC, p3, M1P] 6 times. *12 sts inc; 96 sts.*

Round 19: K8, [p1, k15] 5 times, p1, k7.

Round 20: P6, [2/1/2 RPC, p11] 5 times, 2/1/2 RPC, p5.

Round 21 (inc): [K1, M1, k15, M1] 6 times. *12 sts inc; 108 sts.*

Round 22: P5, [2/2 RPC, p1, 2/2 LPC, p9] 5 times, 2/2 RPC, p1, 2/2 LPC, p4.

Round 23: Knit to end.

Round 24 (inc): [P1, M1P, p2, 2/2 RPC, p5, 2/2 LPC, p2, M1P] 6 times. *12 sts inc; 120 sts.*

Round 25: Knit to end.

Round 26: [P1, 2/3 RPC, p9, 2/3 LPC] 6 times.

Round 27 (inc): K3, [M1, k15, M1, k5] 5 times, M1, k15, M1, pm, sl2, remove marker, return 2 slipped sts to left needle. *12 sts inc; 132 sts.*

Round 28 (dec): [5 into 1[p], p17] 6 times. *24 sts dec; 108 sts.*

Break yarn, leaving tail approx. 40cm [16in] and sl all sts to waste yarn or a stitch holder.

Make a further 5 hexagons (both cowls use the same number of complete hexagons).

Move to step 4.

4 JOINING HEXAGONS

Read Joining Notes at start of pattern (page 71).

SHORT COWL

Join the first 3 hexagons at straight edges to create a 3-hexagon strip, as shown in diagram 1. Ensure that each straight hexagon side has 18 sts.

Join the fourth and fifth hexagons along straight edges as shown in diagram 2, thus making a 2-hexagon strip.

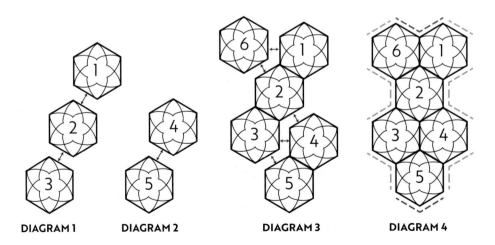

DIAGRAM 1   **DIAGRAM 2**   **DIAGRAM 3**   **DIAGRAM 4**

Slip two sets of 18 sts from adjacent edges of hexagons 1 and 2 in the 3-hexagon strip to your needles and join them to 36 sts from the edge of hexagon 6, as shown in diagram 3.

From your 2-hexagon strip, slip 36 sts from two sides of hexagon 4, and 18 sts from the adjacent side of hexagon 5 to a spare needle. From your 3-hexagon strip, slip 36 sts from two sides of hexagon 3 and 18 sts from the adjacent side of hexagon 2 to another needle, and join the two strips together as shown in diagram 3.

All 6 hexagons are now joined in one piece. Join the cowl to form a loop by slipping 36 sts from 2 sides of hexagon 5 to a spare needle, and slip 18 sts each from adjacent sides of hexagons 6 and 1 to another needle. Join to form a loop as indicated by the red dashed line in diagram 4. The blue dashed lines indicate where the side half-hexagons will be knitted on to complete the sides of the cowl. You will have 4 sets of 54 sts on holders remaining for these side half-hexagons, and 4 sets of 18 sts at the edges of full hexagons, ready for i-cord edging.

For charted instructions move to step 5, for written instructions move to step 6.

LONG COWL

Slip 18 sts from one side of hexagon 1 and 18 sts from one side of hexagon 2 to spare needles and join to create a 2-hexagon strip as shown in diagram 5. Rep this process with hexagons 3 and 4, and hexagons 5 and 6 so that you have three 2-hexagon strips.

Slipping 18 sts to a spare needle for each side to be joined, join the 2-hexagon strips to create one long strip as shown in diagram 6.

Join the cowl to form a loop by slipping 18 sts from the side of hexagon 6 and 18 sts from the side of hexagon 1 to spare needles. Join to form a loop as indicated by the red dashed line in diagram 7. The blue dashed lines indicate where the side half-hexagons will be knitted on to complete the sides of the cowl. You will have 6 sets of 54 sts on holders remaining for these side half-hexagons, and 6 sets of 18 sts at the edges of full hexagons, ready for i-cord edging.

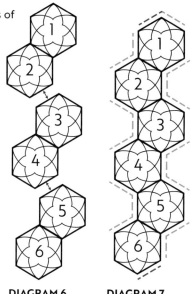

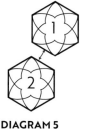

DIAGRAM 5   **DIAGRAM 6**   **DIAGRAM 7**

For charted instructions move to step 5, for written instructions move to step 6.

5 KNITTING ON THE SIDE HALF-HEXAGONS CHARTED INSTRUCTIONS
Half-hexagons are used to fill in the gaps between the attached hexagons. In one of these gaps, with RS facing and using short circular needle, sl 54 sts from waste yarn to needle (18 sts from each available hexagon edge). *54 sts.*

Join in main yarn.
Set-up row (WS): P18, pick up and knit 1 st at corner, p18, pick up and knit 2 sts at corner, p18. *3 sts inc; 57 sts.*
Row 1 (RS, inc): Reading from right to left, work across row 1 of chart B, rep marked section twice. *11 sts inc; 68 sts.*
Row 2 (WS, dec): Reading from left to right, work across row 2 of chart B, rep marked section twice. *6 sts dec; 62 sts remain.*
Last 2 rows set chart B pattern. Cont to work from chart B until row 17 is complete. *41 sts dec; 21 sts remain.*

Row 18 (WS): Sl1 wyif, knit to end.
Row 19 (RS, dec): Sl1 wyif, [p1, p2tog] 6 times, p1, k1. *6 sts dec; 15 sts remain.*
Row 20: Rep row 18.
Row 21 (dec): Sl1 wyif, p2, p3tog, [p1, p3tog] twice, k1. *6 sts dec; 9 sts remain.*
Row 22: Rep row 18.
Row 23 (dec): Sl1 wyif, p2tog, p3tog, p2tog, k1. *4 sts dec; 5 sts remain.*

Break yarn, leaving a short tail and thread through remaining 5 sts on needle. Pull sts tight and weave in end on WS.

Work half-hexagons in remaining gaps along edges between full hexagons. Move to step 7.

6 KNITTING ON THE SIDE HALF-HEXAGONS WRITTEN INSTRUCTIONS
Half-hexagons are used to fill in the gaps between the attached hexagons. In one of these gaps, with RS facing and using short circular needle, sl 54 sts from waste yarn to needle (18 sts from each available hexagon edge). *54 sts.*

Join in main yarn.
Set-up row (WS): P18, pick up and knit 1 st at corner, p18, pick up and knit 2 sts at corner, p18. *3 sts inc; 57 sts.*
Row 1 (RS, inc): Sl1 wyif, kfbf, p17, [1 into 5, p17] twice, kfb, k1. *11 sts inc; 68 sts.*
Row 2 (WS, dec): Sl1 wyif, p2, [ssp, p13, p2tog, p5] twice, ssp, p13, p2tog, p3, k1. *6 sts dec; 62 sts remain.*
Row 3: Sl1 wyif, [p1, 2/3 LPC, p9, 2/3 RPC] 3 times, k1.
Row 4: Sl1 wyif, p60, k1.
Row 5 (dec): Sl1 wyif, [p1, p2tog, p1, 2/2 LPC, p5, 2/2 RPC, p1, ssp] 3 times, k1. *6 sts dec; 56 sts remain.*
Row 6: Sl1 wyif, p54, k1.
Row 7: Sl1 wyif, p5, [2/2 LPC, p1, 2/2 RPC, p9] twice, 2/2 LPC, p1, 2/2 RPC, p4, k1.
Row 8 (dec): Sl1 wyif, [ssp, p13, p2tog, p1] 3 times, k1. *6 sts dec; 50 sts remain.*
Row 9: Sl1 wyif, p6, [2/1/2 RPC, p11] twice, 2/1/2 RPC, p5, k1.
Row 10: Sl1 wyif, p7, [k1, p15] twice, k1, p8, k1.
Row 11 (dec): Sl1 wyif, [p1, p2tog, p2, 2/1 RPC, p1, 2/1 LPC, p2, ssp] 3 times, k1. *6 sts dec; 44 sts remain.*
Row 12: Sl1 wyif, p5, [k3, p11] twice, k3, p6, k1.
Row 13: Sl1 wyif, p3, [2/1 RPC, p3, 2/1 LPC, p5] twice, 2/1 RPC, p3, 2/1 LPC, p2, k1.
Row 14 (dec): Sl1 wyif, [ssp, p2, k5, p2, p2tog, p1] 3 times, k1. *6 sts dec; 38 sts remain.*
Row 15: Sl1 wyif, [p1, 2/1 RPC, p5, 2/1 LPC] 3 times, k1.
Row 16: Sl1 wyif, p2, [k7, p5] twice, k7, p3, k1.

Row 17 (dec): Sl1 wyif, k3tog, p2tog, p3, ssp, [5 into 1[p], p2tog, p3, ssp] twice, ssk, k1. *17 sts dec; 21 sts remain.*
Row 18: Sl1 wyif, knit to end.
Row 19 (dec): Sl1 wyif, [p1, p2tog] 6 times, p1, k1. *6 sts dec; 15 sts remain.*
Row 20: Rep row 18.
Row 21 (dec): Sl1 wyif, p2, p3tog, [p1, p3tog] twice, k1. *6 sts dec; 9 sts remain.*
Row 22: Rep row 18.
Row 23 (dec): Sl1 wyif, p2tog, p3tog, p2tog, k1. *4 sts dec; 5 sts remain.*

Break yarn, leaving a short tail and thread through remaining 5 sts on needle; pull sts tight and weave in end on WS.

Work half-hexagons in remaining gaps along edges between full hexagons. Move to step 7.

7 EDGING
With RS facing, beginning at 18 sts held along one edge of a hexagon, *sl 18 sts from waste yarn to medium or long circular needle, join in yarn and k18, pick up and knit 32 sts along slipped-stitch edge of half-hexagon; rep from * (ignoring reference to 'join in yarn') until sts have been picked up and knitted along one entire edge of cowl. *Short cowl: 100 sts. Long cowl: 150 sts.*

Work an i-cord cast off as follows:
Cast on 4 sts to left needle tip (use your preferred method – cable, knitted or backwards loop are all good choices – or a provisional cast-on for a seamless finish); with RS facing, *k3, ssk, sl4 sts back to left needle; rep from * until all edge sts have been worked. Join ends of i-cord either by undoing provisional cast-on and grafting to final 4 sts; or cast off final 4 sts and seam to cast-on edge.

Rep this step to add the edging on the opposite side of the cowl.

8 FINISHING
Note that when joining the pieces together, small holes may have formed at the points of each hexagon – these can be hidden by weaving in the yarn ends as follows:
With a sharp needle, guide the yarn around the edges of the hole in a circle, catching strands of the work on the WS only, pull tight and weave in to close hole.

Weave in all remaining ends. Soak your cowl in lukewarm water with wool wash for 20–30 minutes. Squeeze out excess water. Lay flat to dry, taking care to arrange the i-cord edging so that it lies straight.

SOMETHING NEW TO LEARN ABOUT **CABLES**

BLANKET

1 MAKE HEXAGONS
Make 22 hexagons, following the instructions in steps 1–3 of the Cowl pattern (page 73).

2 CAST ON FOR HALF-HEXAGONS
Cast on 5 sts using waste yarn and the crochet provisional cast-on method (or your preferred provisional method). Change to main yarn and knit 1 row.

Row 1 (RS, inc): Sl1 wyif, pfb, pfbf, pfb, k1. *4 sts inc; 9 sts.*
Row 2 (WS): Sl1 wyif, knit to end.
Row 3 (inc): Sl1 wyif, [p1, M1P] 6 times, p1, k1. *6 sts inc; 15 sts.*
Row 4: Rep row 2.
Row 5 (inc): Sl1 wyif, p2, [M1P, p2] 5 times, p1, k1. *5 sts inc; 20 sts.*
Row 6: Rep row 2.

For charted instructions move to step 3, for written instructions move to step 4.

3 WORK HALF-HEXAGON CABLE PATTERN CHARTED INSTRUCTIONS
Row 7 (RS, inc): Reading from right to left, work across row 7 of chart C, rep the marked section twice. *18 sts inc; 38 sts.*
Row 8 (WS): Reading from left to right, work across row 8 of chart C, rep the marked section twice.
Last 2 rows set chart C pattern. Cont to work from chart C until row 23 is complete. *18 sts inc; 56 sts.*
The half-hexagon will have 10 sts along each of the half-edges and two sets of 18 sts along the full edges.

Break yarn, leaving tail approx. 40cm [16in] and sl all sts to waste yarn or a stitch holder.

Remove the waste yarn from the cast-on edge and thread the main yarn tail through the sts. Pull tight and weave in the end on the WS.

Make a further 9 half-hexagons in the same way. Move to step 5.

4 WORK HALF-HEXAGON CABLE PATTERN WRITTEN INSTRUCTIONS
Row 7 (RS, inc): Sl1 wyif, p2, M1P, p1, [1 into 5, p1, M1P, p3, M1P, p1] twice, 1 into 5, p1, M1P, p1, k1. *18 sts inc; 38 sts.*
Row 8 (WS): Sl1 wyif, k3, p5, [k7, p5] twice, k5.
Row 9: Sl1 wyif, p3, 2/1 RPC, [p1, 2/1 LPC, p5, 2/1 RPC] twice, p1, 2/1 LPC, p2, k1.
Row 10 (inc): Sl1 wyif, k2, p3, M1P, p1, [M1P, p3, k5, p3, M1P, p1] twice, M1P, p3, k4. *6 sts inc; 44 sts.*
Row 11: Sl1 wyif, p2, 2/1 RPC, p5, [2/1 LPC, p3, 2/1 RPC, p5] twice, 2/1 LPC, p1, k1.
Row 12: Sl1 wyif, k1, [p11, k3] 3 times.
Row 13 (inc): Sl1 wyif, [p1, 2/1 RPC, p3, M1P, p1, M1P, p3, 2/1 LPC] 3 times, k1. *6 sts inc; 50 sts.*
Row 14: Sl1 wyif, [p15, k1] twice, p16, k1.
Row 15: Sl1 wyif, p1, k2, p11, [2/1/2 RPC, p11] twice, k3.
Row 16 (inc): Sl1 wyif, p7, M1P, p1, [M1P, p15, M1P, p1] twice, M1P, p8, k1. *6 sts inc; 56 sts.*
Row 17: Sl1 wyif, [p1, 2/2 LPC, p9, 2/2 RPC] 3 times, k1.
Row 18: Sl1 wyif, p54, k1.
Row 19 (inc): Sl1 wyif, p3, 2/2 LPC, p2, M1P, [p1, M1P, p2, 2/2 RPC, p5, 2/2 LPC, p2, M1P] twice, p1, M1P, p2, 2/2 RPC, p2, k1. *6 sts inc; 62 sts.*
Row 20: Sl1 wyif, p60, k1.
Row 21: Sl1 wyif, p5, 2/3 LPC, [p1, 2/3 RPC, p9, 2/3 LPC] twice, p1, 2/3 RPC, p4, k1.
Row 22 (inc): Sl1 wyif, p7, M1P, p5, [M1P, p15, M1P, p5] twice, M1P, p8, k1. *6 sts inc; 68 sts.*
Row 23 (dec): Sl1 wyif, p9, [5 into 1[p], p17] twice, 5 into 1[p], p8, k1. *12 sts dec; 56 sts remain.*

KEY

☐   Knit on RS, purl on WS

⊡   Purl on RS, knit on WS

Ⓜ   M1 on RS, M1P on WS

Ⓜ   M1P on RS

🅐   5 into 1[p]

Ⅴ   1 into 5

Ⅴ   Sl1 pwise wyif

☐   Pattern repeat

2/1 RPC slip 1 st to cable needle and hold at back, k2; p1 from cable needle

2/1 LPC slip 2 sts to cable needle and hold at front, p1; k2 from cable needle

2/2 RPC slip 2 sts to cable needle and hold at back, k2; p2 from cable needle

2/2 LPC slip 2 sts to cable needle and hold at front, p2; k2 from cable needle

2/1/2 RPC slip 3 sts to cable needle and hold at back, k2; return left-hand st from cable needle to left needle, p1; k2 from cable needle

2/3 LPC slip 2 sts to cable needle and hold at front, p3; k2 from cable needle

2/3 RPC slip 3 sts to cable needle and hold at back, k2; p3 from cable needle

CHART C
BLANKET EDGE HALF-HEXAGONS

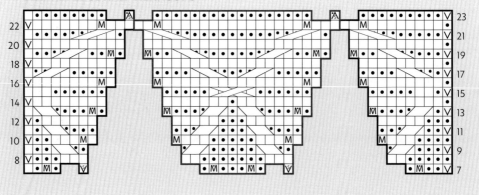

The half-hexagon will have 10 sts along each of the half-edges and two sets of 18 sts along the full edges.
Break yarn, leaving tail approx. 40cm [16in] and sl all sts to waste yarn or a stitch holder.

Remove the waste yarn from the cast-on edge and thread the main yarn tail through the sts. Pull tight and weave in the end on the WS.

Make a further 9 half-hexagons in the same way. Move to step 5.

5 JOINING HEXAGONS
Reading Joining Notes at start of pattern (page 71).

Slipping 18 sts from one side of a hexagon each time, join first 4 hexagons at straight edges as shown in diagram 8.

Make 2 further 4-hexagon strips in the same way.

Slipping 18 sts from one side of a hexagon each time, join 5 hexagons at straight edges in exactly the same way. Make 1 further 5-hexagon strip.

Join a 4-hexagon strip to a 5-hexagon strip as shown in diagram 9, slipping 144 sts to a spare needle along each side of the strips.

Cont to join 144 sts along each side of alternating 4- and 5-hexagon strips according to diagram 10.

DIAGRAM 8

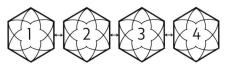

DIAGRAM 9

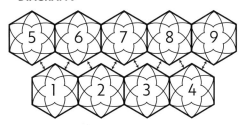

DIAGRAM 10

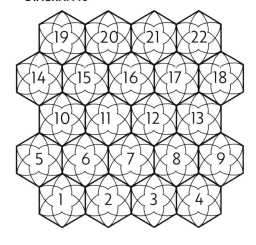

PROJECT **PLEIONE BLANKET**

Slipping 10 sts from the half-sides of the half-hexagons each time, join 5 half-hexagons to form a strip as shown in diagram 11. Make a further 5-half-hexagon strip in the same way.

Join the 5-half-hexagon strips to each end of the blanket by slipping 144 sts to a spare needle along each side, as shown in diagram 12.

The blue dashed lines indicate where the side half-hexagons will be knitted on to complete the sides of the blanket. You will have 6 sets of 54 sts on holders remaining for these side half-hexagons, as well as 4 sets of 10 sts at the edges of half-hexagons and 4 sets of 18 sts at the edges of full hexagons, ready for i-cord edging.

DIAGRAM 11

DIAGRAM 12

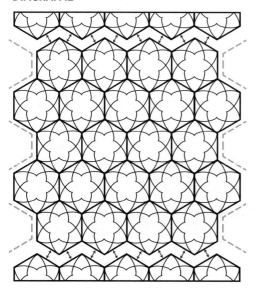

6 KNITTING ON THE SIDE HALF-HEXAGONS
Knit half-hexagons into the 6 gaps at the sides of the blanket, following step 5 of the Cowl for charted instructions (page 76), and step 6 of the Cowl for written instructions (page 76).

7 EDGING
**With RS facing, beginning at corner of blanket (with chart C edge to right and charts A and B edge to left), sl 10 sts from waste yarn to long circular needle, join in yarn and kfbf, k9, *pick up and knit 36 sts along slipped-stitch edge of half-hexagon, sl 18 sts from waste yarn to circular needle, k18; rep from * once more, pick up and knit 36 sts along slipped st edge of half-hexagon, sl 10 sts from waste yarn to circular needle and k9, kfbf. *168 sts along first edge of blanket.*

With RS still facing, [along slipped-stitch edge of each half-hexagon, pick up and knit 34 sts] 5 times. *170 sts along second edge of blanket.* **

Rep from ** to ** to work sts along third and fourth edges of blanket. *676 sts.*

Cast on 4 sts to left needle (from RS use cable or knitted cast-on, or turn to WS and use backwards loop cast-on or provisional cast-on for a seamless finish); with RS facing, *k3, ssk, sl4 sts back to left needle; rep from * until all edge sts have been worked. At each corner of blanket work an extra row of i-cord without attaching (k4, sl4 sts back to left needle), to ease around corner.

Join ends of i-cord either by undoing provisional cast-on and grafting to final 4 sts; or cast off final 4 sts and seam to cast-on edge.

8 FINISHING
Note that when joining the pieces together, small holes may have formed at the points of each hexagon – these can be hidden by weaving in the yarn ends as follows:
With a sharp needle, guide the yarn around the edges of the hole in a circle, catching strands of the work on the WS only, pull tight and weave in to close hole.

Weave in all remaining ends. Soak your blanket in lukewarm water with wool wash for 20–30 minutes. Squeeze out excess water. Lay flat to dry, taking care to arrange the i-cord edging so that it lies straight.

SOMETHING NEW TO LEARN ABOUT **CABLES**

SOMETHING NEW TO LEARN ABOUT **CABLES**

YARN

When working cables, yarn choice is important – it must be a smooth, springy yarn in solid, or semi-solid colours to show off the cables most effectively.

If a yarn lacks an inherent springiness, the manipulation that the stitches undergo can leave them overstretched, whereas a yarn that bounces back into shape is ideal.

A smooth yarn that gives the best possible stitch definition will ensure that your cables pop out of the fabric, allowing them to really shine.

Colours should be solid or semi-solid since variegation will distract the eye from the surface texture of your stitches.

All of the patterns and tutorials in this volume use Coop Knits Socks Yeah! DK. We have selected this yarn in particular because it fulfils all the requirements for showcasing the best from your cables.

The blend of different coloured fibres in each colour gives an overall shade with great depth and complexity while still giving well-defined cables.

Socks Yeah! DK is a smooth, springy blend of wool and nylon, ensuring that your cabled hand knits will look great and wear well for many years to come.

TENSION

Tension (US gauge) information is given for all projects. If you don't match tension with the recommended needle size, try again with smaller or larger needles as required. Yarn quantity used and finished size are determined by matching tension correctly.

WHERE TO FIND US?

You can follow Jen and Jim on...

RAVELRY	**JenACKnitwear / VeufTricot**
FACEBOOK	**Arnall-Culliford Knitwear**
INSTAGRAM	**@jenacknitwear / @veuftricot**
TWITTER	**@jenacknitwear / @veuftricot**
YOUTUBE	**JenACKnitwear**
OUR BLOG	**www.acknitwear.co.uk/blog**

Visit **www.acknitwear.co.uk** to see our full range of books, yarns and other knitting accessories.

SUPPORT

If you require help with any of the techniques, or patterns, do join us in our friendly group on Ravelry at Arnall-Culliford Knitwear (**www.ravelry.com/groups/arnall-culliford-knitwear**). You may find your question has already been asked, and if not, there are lots of helpful and friendly knitters around to assist you. Your question may also help others, so please don't hesitate to post to our group.

DOWNLOAD

For technical assistance with your purchase of *Something New to Learn About Cables*, please email **jim@acknitwear.co.uk**.

VIDEO TUTORIALS

We have created video tutorials to accompany *Something New to Learn About Cables*, and they can all be found on our website at:
www.acknitwear.co.uk/something-new-to-learn-about-cables

You will also find a selection of general video tutorials on our website:
www.acknitwear.co.uk/tutorials-1

1 into 5	with yarn at back of work, *insert right needle between first 2 stitches on left needle, wrap yarn around right needle and pull through to make a stitch, slip first stitch on left needle to right needle, insert left needle between first 2 stitches on right needle, wrap yarn around left needle and pull through to make a stitch*, slip first stitch on right needle to left needle; rep from * to * once more, slip 2 stitches from left needle to right needle (4 stitches increased)
1/1 LPC	slip 1 stitch to cable needle and hold at front, p1; k1 from cable needle
1/1 RPC	slip 1 stitch to cable needle and hold at back, k1; p1 from cable needle
2/1 LPC	slip 2 stitches to cable needle and hold at front, p1; k2 from cable needle
2/1 RC	slip 1 stitch to cable needle and hold at back, k2; k1 from cable needle
2/1 RPC	slip 1 stitch to cable needle and hold at back, k2; p1 from cable needle
2/1/2 RPC	slip 3 stitches to cable needle and hold at back, k2; return left-hand stitch from cable needle to left needle, p1; k2 from cable needle
2/2 LC	slip 2 stitches to cable needle and hold at front, k2; k2 from cable needle
2/2 LPC	slip 2 stitches to cable needle and hold at front, p2; k2 from cable needle
2/2 RC	slip 2 stitches to cable needle and hold at back, k2; k2 from cable needle

2/2 RPC	slip 2 stitches to cable needle and hold at back, k2; p2 from cable needle
2/2/2 LPC	slip 2 stitches to cable needle and hold in front, slip next 2 stitches to a second cable needle and hold at back, k2; p2 from back cable needle; k2 from front cable needle
2/2/2 RPC	slip 4 stitches to cable needle and hold at back, k2; slip left-hand 2 stitches from cable needle to left needle, p2; k2 from cable needle
2/3 LPC	slip 2 stitches to cable needle and hold at front, p3; k2 from cable needle
2/3 RPC	slip 3 stitches to cable needle and hold at back, k2; p3 from cable needle
5 into 1[p]	slip next 3 stitches to right needle, pass second slipped stitch over first stitch on right needle and off needle; slip stitch from right needle back to left needle and pass second stitch on left needle over first stitch and off needle; slip stitch from left needle to right needle and pass second stitch over first stitch and off needle; slip remaining stitch on right needle back to left needle and pass second stitch on left needle over first stitch and off needle; purl remaining stitch (4 stitches decreased)

cont	continue(d)/continues/continuing
dec	decrease(d)/decreases/decreasing
foll	follow(s)/following
inc	increase(d)/increases/increasing
k	knit
k2tog	knit next 2 stitches together (1 stitch decreased)
k3tog	knit next 3 stitches together (2 stitches decreased)
kfb	knit into front and back of next stitch (1 stitch increased)
kfbf	knit into front, back and front of next stitch (2 stitches increased)
M1	as M1L
M1L	make 1 stitch by lifting the bar between stitches from front to back and knitting into the back of this loop (1 stitch increased)
M1P	make 1 stitch by lifting the bar between stitches from front to back and purling into the back of this loop (1 stitch increased)
M1R	make 1 stitch by lifting the bar between stitches from back to front and knitting into the front of this loop (1 stitch increased)
p	purl
p2tog	purl next 2 stitches together (1 stitch decreased)
p3tog	purl next 3 stitches together (2 stitches decreased)
pfb	purl into front and back of next stitch (1 stitch increased)
pfbf	purl into front, back and front of next stitch (2 stitches increased)
pm	place marker
pwise	purlwise
rep	repeat(s)/repeating
RS	right side
sl	slip stitch(es) purlwise, unless otherwise stated
slm	slip marker

ssk	slip 1 stitch knitwise, slip 1 stitch purlwise (or knitwise), return both stitches to left needle without twisting and knit them together through the back loop (1 stitch decreased)
ssp	slip next 2 stitches knitwise, separately, return both stitches to left needle without twisting and purl them together through the back loop (1 stitch decreased)
st(s)	stitch(es)
WS	wrong side
wyib	with yarn in back
wyif	with yarn in front

**ALSO AVAILABLE FROM
ARNALL-CULLIFORD KNITWEAR:**

Information

THE TEAM

JEN ARNALL-CULLIFORD
In demand as a meticulous editor of knitting patterns for others, Jen is sometimes tempted into creating her own designs. She has an encyclopaedic knowledge of knitting techniques, and has written all of the tutorials in this volume.

JIM ARNALL-CULLIFORD
Jim is somewhat bemused by the turn life has taken of late – editing and designing knitwear wasn't where he thought his chemistry degree would lead him!

NIC BLACKMORE **Art and Production Editor**
Nic brings our designs and tutorials to life through her thoughtful layout and design. She is also the best virtual office mate in the world.

JESSE WILD **Photographer**
When he isn't photographing cycling and rock legends, Jesse can be found ensuring every stitch of the knitwear is in focus, and filming our video tutorials. He always brings a giggle to shoot days.   *www.jessewild.co.uk*

SALLY SOMERS **Chief Knit-picker**
Between teaching kids how to checkmate with a lawnmower and bringing consistency and clarity to the nation's cookbooks, Sally has found time to turn her hand to knitting, and combed the text of this book for anomalies.

RACHEL COOPEY **Designer**
Rachel lives and breathes sock design, and her patterns are packed with clever stitch combinations and beautiful features. When she's not knitting socks, she also creates amazing accessory patterns. Rachel has now published four sock pattern books, and two accessory collections, including the *Coop Knits Socks* and *Coop Knits Toasty* series.
www.coopknits.co.uk

LUCY HAGUE **Designer**
Lucy's designs draw on her fascination with Pictish and Celtic artwork, and she is a master at reimagining complex knotwork into knitted cables. Her patterns often use unusual stitches that she has created. Lucy has published two pattern books of her intricate designs: *Celtic Cable Shawls* and *Illuminated Knits*.   *www.lucyhague.co.uk*

ACKNOWLEDGEMENTS

Many thanks to the team at Cooper Hall in Frome for allowing us to use their beautiful grounds for our photo shoot.

Grateful thanks to Rachel and Lucy, not only for contributing their wonderful designs, but also for being such good fun on the photo shoot.

Jesse and Janet Wild were kind enough to allow us to use their home for photography – we are very grateful! With thanks also to Janet and Moomin for extra modelling.

To Sheila Gore, Maylin Scott and Katherine Smoak, for their accurate and speedy sample knitting, huge thanks are due.

Our Ravelry group continues to be a source of inspiration and supportive camaraderie. Many thanks to everyone who participates, but particularly to Alix, Katherine, Maylin and Nancy for being so generous with their precious time in supporting us as moderators.

Finally, my local knitting group in Frome are a constant rock, and I couldn't do it without you. Thank you all!